Someday mija,
you'll learn
the difference
between a whore
and a
working woman

Someday Mija, You'll Learn the Difference Between a Whore and a Working Woman

a memoir

Yvonne Martinez

SHE WRITES PRESS

Published 2022
Printed in the United States of America
Print ISBN: 978-1-64742-102-1
E-ISBN: 978-1-64742-103-8
Library of Congress Control Number: 2022908418

For information, address:
She Writes Press
1569 Solano Ave #546
Berkeley, CA 94707

Interior design by Tabitha Lahr

She Writes Press is a division of SparkPoint Studio, LLC.

I dedicate this book to all the *tal Marías*
who dare to love and be loved.

And to my late sister, Belinda María Martinez Steele,
whose writing journey was just beginning.

DISHES AND DOLLS

On the first morning of her death, she lay with her arms wide and her palms facing heaven. Flat on her back under the bay window, it looked like she had fallen from the bed that was too big for the tiny Victorian dining room where she slept.

That first morning was the beginning of my search. A search that would lead me to secrets inside secrets to a truth that broke out on its own. It came out bit by bit, at times too heavy to handle, but eventually I became strong enough to hold this much of it. That first morning of her death, her life ended, but her story began.

Each morning her feet touched down on the warm wood, and in just six barefoot paces she could get to the four-burner stove in the skinny kitchen for a light and then back to the edge of her bed by the window.

Between long drags of her Salem menthol, she'd sit and look out from ten floors up over a sliver of San Francisco that would become Japantown. When the six paces to the stove got too hard (she refused to have matches or lighters by her bed because they were a hazard), she'd call out to me, "Ivana!" her name for me, her granddaughter, Yvonne. She'd call me from wherever I was to light her cigarettes at all hours of the day and night.

When I found her that morning, her head was on the wood inlay, where the natural gold-and-yellow wood met slat to slat, plank edge to plank edge in fixed angles, gold against brown. Grandma Mary had managed to pull down a sheet as she fell. It gathered cross-crooked over her short torso under the light of the bay window.

Even in the light, she didn't look like herself. There were no rings on her fingers, no "real red" lipstick, no black pencil eyebrows drawn over her eyes with the shiny Maybelline shaved-tip pencil she'd wet her lips with before drawing the arches over her eyelids. Instead, her yellow, cigarette-burnt fingers curved into a half curl and lay parallel to her hips. The chipped red paint on her toes pointed east and west. Her eyes were half-closed; her gaze was gone.

She told no one she was dying. But they all knew, the absent man, the missing cat, and her no-show son. One by one, as she'd gotten sicker and sicker, they'd all taken off.

Grandma was living by herself by the time I got there. I'd been planning a run from my mother's house ever since the Salt Lake City police installed me there in kindergarten. By the second grade, my stepfather had moved us all to Los Angeles, far, far away from my mother's family and everything Utah. Each time I ran, I'd gotten farther away. I didn't begin to make real breaks for it until I was fifteen. This time I'd made it as far as San Francisco, all the way to Mary's.

The free clinic movement drew her west from Salt Lake to San Francisco when she got sick.

As I knelt over her, I never fathomed that she was actually dead. I left her on the floor undisturbed, gathered my robe around me, and went into the four-by-four foyer that separated our two rooms.

Where Mexican grandmothers put candles and saints in their alcoves, Grandma Mary stationed a heavy black telephone on top of the white and yellow pages. There was no blinking Jesus; no plug-in off and on sacred hearts; no benevolent, blue-shrouded Virgin Mary—only heavy black metal.

I lifted the phone receiver only to feel it drop in my wrist like a free weight. The coil rolled itself tightly around the base of the phone. I put my finger in the black metal cutout dial marked "0" and pulled it all the way around. The dial rolled over the numbers on the phone's face and took its tick-tick time getting back to zero. I spoke into the receiver close and low, perched in the alcove like I was in a confessional booth.

"Something's wrong with my grandmother," I said.

"We'll send someone," a voice said back.

"She's on the floor and won't move," I said.

"We'll send someone," the voice repeated.

It felt like a screen slat closed shut at the end of a confession when the call ended. There was only silence, not even the comfort of a string of penance in the wake of the shut sound. Nothing in my hands, nothing to hold on to.

The morning light started to shift away from the wood pattern around Grandma's head, and still no one came. I called the voice in the alcove and called again, walked back and forth to the window, finally pushed it open toward the street and propped open the front door to look down the narrow hallway to see if anybody had arrived to rescue her in the way that you believe that magic will happen just by calling the doctor.

Everybody, it seemed, knew that she was dead but me. I pulled my robe tighter around me and took the accordion door elevator down to the street to see if the ambulance was coming. In the pink, faux fur–lined slippers that she'd given me, I tiptoed across the lobby and out the front of the building. I pulled the pink belt of my matching robe around my waist, the line of pink faux fur crisscrossing over my breasts. My arms wrapped around myself, I stood at the top of the granite steps and took one long look up Post Street and down the other way.

Back inside, the heavy, wood-sculpted door pushed me back into the lobby. My pink fur heels click-clacked across the black-and-white octagon tiles to the elevator. I took one last look through the beveled glass and saw cat paws and hiking boots. My uncle was coming up the steps from around the corner with Grandma's missing cat. I pushed the door open, wide enough for him, the cat, and his bedroll backpack. My other arm closed my robe over me.

"Uncle," I said.

"Hey, kid," he said.

"Where've you been?" I asked.

He pulled the red bandanna off his head and snapped it into the air.

"Here," he said.

Snap.

"And there," he said.

Snap. Snap.

"She's been on the floor for hours and won't move," I said.

Uncle slid the accordion elevator door shut in front of us and tied the bandanna around his wrist. He pulled it tight with his teeth. I folded my arms over the pink fur of my robe.

"I called the ambulance hours ago," I said.

I took the key that I found gripped in my hand and opened the door to the apartment. My uncle dropped his backpack just inside the tiny foyer under the phone alcove, leaving the pack ready for remount. He pulled one of his fingerless gloves off his hand with his teeth and took one step toward Grandma's bedroom in the dining room. In just three steps, he bowed his head under the Victorian circle block corner doorway, his hair in tight black curls around his face. He stood over her with his tip-less gloves hanging out of his back pocket.

He rubbed the sweat of his palms onto the thighs of his hiking shorts. "Let's take a look," he said.

He squatted on the window side of her and pressed his hands

deeper into his thighs; his boots over the even light-and-dark patterned wood, he bent over her.

"María," he said in a short breath to himself. Not calling to her, he simply named her. He pushed in on the flesh of her cheek with his hitchhiking thumb.

"María," he said.

Her brown face went gray against the red bandanna on his wrist. Her head just hung in his hand, as it fell to the side when he released it.

"María," he said.

Uncle stood up, took a step back, rubbed his hands deeper into his thighs, then reached over her. With one swift yank, he pulled her sheet up from her feet up over her torso. The sheet landed over her face and exposed her from the waist down.

"Take a good look," he said.

Her short legs opened to graying pubic hair.

"That's all she was," he said.

His face twisted into one word.

Cunt.

He wiped his forehead with the red bandanna around his wrist.

"That's all she ever was to me," he said.

He moved away from her in the same three steps he took crab-like to get to her.

"That's all," he repeated.

Near naked under the robe she had given me, I could only hold my arms tighter over my breasts.

He filled his arms with all her favorite candles, the big ones and the small ones, the half-melted ones, the wide purple ones, the scented ones, the untouched white ones wrapped in tissue in the drawer, plus her blue dishes, all her dolls, and her red geraniums.

"It's time to get rid of all this shit," he said.

Back and forth down the skinny hallway he went. He left a trail of dirt, broken candles, and red petals on his way to the garbage chute. He stuffed and stuffed until the chute's metal door couldn't close. When there was no more room, he piled up dishes, dolls, clothes, and anything else he could along the wall under the half-open metal chute. Broken pieces of Grandma's things fell Picasso-like into a shrine and refracted light from broken pictures gathered under the heap.

Nothing could interrupt my uncle's tight lips and the ridges of wrinkled skin on his forehead, a hate that got shinier with sweat with every load he carried. When there was no more room in and around the chute to shove things, he pressed his back against the kitchen wall and slid to the floor across from the stove, just steps from where Grandma lay. He loosened his hiking boots, rested his elbow on his bent knee, and looked over at her. All the dishes were gone, her pots, her collections of mismatched saltshakers, her clothes, everything. Everything went down that chute, even her pillow and the blankets on her bed. There was nothing left to shove down the chute but her.

She lay near naked, alone and dead from uterine cancer at fifty-two, exposed in death in a way that she'd spent her whole life trying to avoid. I pulled the sheet back down from her face and over her legs.

When the coroner came that evening, Uncle was gone. The ambulance gurney's legs flipped down under its metal frame beside Grandma where she lay under the bay window. The coroner had her body lifted hand to hand into a long black bag, way too big for her tiny frame. He joined the heavy metal zipper near her feet. With one long yank, he pulled the silver teeth over her short legs, her flattened breasts, and her face. Hand to hand, he had her lifted one more time onto the gurney and with it made his way through the hallway, rolling her over her red petals and dirt, broken candles and blue dishes, doll arms and legs, to the elevator and down to the street.

At nearly nineteen, my body already knew what there was to know about my grandmother. Knew it in ways I didn't yet have words for. Knew it in the binary neutron charges that informed my posture, my language, and my bearing in the world and told of it in ways that I didn't know that I knew.

The only thing that mattered to me in the days that led up that morning was that she had taken me in and now she was gone.

Now, nearly fifty years later, I have been able to put together the years of veiled references, coded phrases, and hidden asides to reveal the reason for my family's open contempt for my grandmother. When I finally did hear the words, heard my aunt speak them out loud, they were the last layer of confirmation, the last piece of evidence. They were hearsay as good as any primary source. And even then, I had to store them away until I could find a safe place to examine them, to bring them out. Words that began in the phrases and images etched in me since I was a little girl in Salt Lake City where I lived with my grandma Mary's mother, my great-grandmother Mercedes Murillo Corona, and her second husband, my grandfather, Vidal Corona, whose real name wasn't Corona, it was Arguelles. He wasn't who he said he was. His name and my mother's parentage were only a few of the many secrets that my family protected.

CHAPTER 1

FUNERALS

When she wasn't praying for the dead babies, Great-Grandma Mercedes crashed Salt Lake funerals wherever she could, but mostly at Our Lady of Guadalupe Catholic Church. "*Incate*," she said.

At six, I'd learned to kneel under the golden holy water bowl. The hem of my dress, eyes of white eyelet, the tiny holes in white embossed cotton, brushed across the fat blue flower tiles. I pulled off the white gloves she insisted I wear and laid them across the gold edges of my missal. I pulled my pink plastic rosary out of my white shoulder purse one bead at a time. I put the gloves back in my purse to leave white fingertips hanging out the side of it. My knees on the tile, my bare wrist over the edge of the holy water bowl, I wet my fingers to lay drops on my forehead, my heart, my left shoulder, my right shoulder, and with what was left of the wet, I touched my lips.

I walked one step behind Mercedes and tried not to step directly on the blue flowers. When she paused, I paused. When she stopped, I stopped. When she genuflected midway before the sanctuary and crossed herself, I genuflected and crossed myself.

When finally, we entered the second pew on the left side of the church, there stood a statue of San Martín de Porres. We balanced our backsides against the edge of the wooden pew while Mercedes pulled down the red kneeler and our knees went down on the sticky dark-red plastic. Mercedes's fat black wooden beads bunched in her hand. She made little crosses at each station of her body with one big cross over all of her, a cross over all the crosses, top to bottom, left to right, and then she lifted the metal crucifix to her lips for a long, closed-eyed kiss. Hers was the long way, the Mexican way.

The sky-blue casket lay in state in the middle of the aisle just outside the sculpted white marble ballast that separated the pews from the altar.

The deceased man's gray mustache had been painted black to match his painted black hair. His skin was a deep, almost copper, tan. His sideburns and Tin-Tan-like mustache was barber cut so you could see the shadow of shaved hair along the Mexican lines of his face. His brown flesh lay in folds over his white collar; only the wild gray in his eyebrows let you see him without elaboration.

I'd crashed a lot of funerals of people I didn't know with my great-grandmother, so the corpses seemed more like curiosities to me than real dead people.

Incense came at us in torrents from a ball-shaped, silver clapper cast out at us from a long chain. White smoke twisted, turned, and burned the insides of my nose, mouth, and throat. Only the scent of the dozens of roses on the casket let me breathe. Above us, the monstrance with its single bull's-eye mirror sent out rays in rippled gold.

The life-size statue of San Martín de Porres stood in his corner, a white baby lamb in his arms. His hair and robes were black and white; his hands and face were a dark brown like mine. Mercedes always sat near him in the funerals we crashed and said words to him soft and familiar, like he was her paisano,

2

her sentry in the outlands of Utah where we lived far away from anything Mexican. In another corner of the church, the triangle baby saint held court. With a little diamond crown on its head, it wore a blue-and-gold brocade gown that flowed from its neck into a triangle, and it held a child-sized staff in its porcelain hand.

"*Aquí vas a conocer la verdad*," Mercedes said.

Funerals were where the real stories are told, she said, where people gathered to mock the public lie told about themselves and the deceased.

Mercedes's hands were wrapped tightly in her fat wooden rosary, tight enough for blood to gather red in her hands. The more she prayed, the tighter she pulled. The tighter she pulled, the faster she prayed. The faded black beads tapped against the pew in front of us as her body moved up and back with her breath. Covered head to shoulders, Mercedes's long black-and-gold veil brushed gold lace against her brown cheeks.

At the end of a mystery, joyful or sorrowful, I never knew which, Mercedes lifted her head and pointed herself in the direction of a woman in the pew a row up and across the dead man's aisle from us. The woman's face was covered by an all-black veil that was long enough to crisscross in front at the woman's neck and fold into black lace scallops over each of her shoulders. I could only see the silhouette of her face and the curves of gold earrings through black organza. Mercedes pulled a fat bead through her hand and nodded to the woman.

"*Esa.*"

Her fingers pushed out another bead.

"*Esa, es la esposa*," she said.

His wife.

In the pew directly in front of us, a young woman in a narrow black dress stood. Her veil stopped above her bare shoulders, and her skirt stopped at her knees. Her long legs were covered in black stockings, and she wore black heels. Mercedes nodded to her.

3

"*Acá está la hija*," she said.

Over here is the daughter.

Next to the dead man's daughter stood a woman who wore a black-and-silver veil, her beads tap-tapping against her pew.

"*La otra mujer*," she said.

The other woman, the deceased's outside wife.

Across the aisle from their sister, the adult sons of the dead man stood on either side of their mother with the shoulders of their black suits against the black lace scallops of their mother's organza veil. The son nearest the middle aisle wore a neat cut Tee-Square goatee. He lifted his head and turned to look across the aisle that separated him from his half-sister. His sister parted her red lipstick lips to send him back a smile. He lowered his head and stalked his foot on the red kneeler like a pony.

Children stood parallel to children, their mothers on either side of them in contrasting black-and-silver veils. Only the aisle that led to the dead man separated them.

All facing God.

When someone dies, Mercedes said in words as soft as her prayers, all the entangled attachments are exposed. Every way the dead person knew love or was loved is revealed. Only when dead can we truly know how the dead person loved.

Mercedes pushed fat wooden beads through her hands, prayer after prayer. When she finished, she pressed her bead-wrapped hand against mine and pulled me past Jesus on the cross with his crown of thorns, blood down the sides of his face, blood on his hands, and blood on his feet. Only a small cloth to cover him.

She pulled me right by Jesus, like he wasn't there. We passed him to rows and rows of red glass candles to another shrine. Burning wax smelled and lit liquid pools around flickering wicks. The corner of candles smelled the heavy smell that wells inside like camphor and black shawls.

Mercedes found a fresh wax wick, put her penny in the small black metal box for a match, lit it, and knelt down on the padless kneeler. My knees hit the bony wooden slats in front of a statue of a woman in a blue shroud who had a serpent at her feet.

"*Santa María, Madre de Dios, reza por nosotros . . . Santa María . . .*"

Somewhere in the middle of her prayers, she started to talk to him.

"*Vengo hablarte, Cirilo. No se adonde to llevaron, esposo mio querido. Te he estado buscando desde que te rostraron muerto y sin cabeza por todo el pueblo. Te he estado buscando para saber adonde te llevaron. No me dejaron enterarte, perdí el niño, y murió la hija que no conociste.*"

That's when I first heard her talk to him, at the funerals we crashed. He, who she couldn't find. He, who she never got to bury. He, who they dragged headless through town after they shot him. He, who she told over and over about the dead babies: the little boy who died and his namesake, the dead little girl he never knew.

CHAPTER 2

THE DEAD BABIES

With their pink cheeks, full bellies, and blond curls, Great-Grandma Mercedes put the gilded holy card cherubs next to a holy card picture of a throbbing red heart. She put them on the fireplace mantle, opposite the bay windows where Salt Lake winter fell against three-paneled glass in seamless white sheets. The holy card heart's fluted blue veins, truncated valves, and cutoff arteries didn't need a body. It beat on its own.

Cherub arms and plump fingers lifted open hands up to heaven against an unreal blue holy card sky. The babies and the heart faced each other in a forest of standing thin, short, tall, white, pink, blue, and black candles and of melted wax that hung over the fireplace mantle like stalactites. The wax forest clearing made way for a toy rocking horse, a package of dried shrimp, my birthday cake ballerinas, cinnamon sticks, hard butterscotch candies, sea horses, and dried red rosebuds.

There was something else in the shrine for the dead babies that my great-grandmother Mercedes tended, something I knew was there but couldn't see, something hiding in plain sight.

A picture of the first dead baby.

Inside the top half of the white baby casket, cream-colored satin folded into pleats in a dome over the head of the little boy who lay there. His tiny brown face was stretched and taut like that of a mummy. Satin clouds made pillows under his head. His eyelids were closed and his forehead flat, his left forefinger placed over his right hand. In death, each side of him rested against its opposite, his body in balance for the last time. Eyeball-close, he was laid out in white baptism clothes. But he was dead.

We never knew him, only his name and the stories told about him, the first of the three Utah dead babies. The second dead baby had a name and a story, but no picture. The third dead baby had no picture, and no name or story until I found her.

The little boy in the picture was my mother's dead brother.

Mother told her own stories about the dead babies. Always with her back turned while she leaned and pressed into a mound of dough kneaded together from flour, lard, salt, and water—a mound big enough to feed eleven of us. Dough stuck to her hands and hardened into her cuticles. She rubbed off the moist dough that stuck between her fingers and wiped the sticky wads against a stained flour sack that she pinned over her workday dress, a sleeveless paisley shift that closed in the back with a button on top instead of a zipper.

Mother's broomstick rolling pin pace got faster with her story-telling, her paisley against the rippled chrome that surrounded our yellow Formica, the kitchen table in the middle of the kitchen. The clacks of her rolling pin slammed on top on a fist-sized mound of dough that she'd torn off and lined up in rows a dozen at a time. She then slammed it into a circle, lifted it, slapped it twice, turned it, and rolled it into a wider circle until it was ready for the griddle.

Clack, clack, turn.

"In those days," Mother started. "In those days, funerals were at home and the people came to the house for the wake," she said.

Clack, clack, turn.

My Catholic school uniform was of no use in the after-school smog-heavy LA heat. The wool in my red pleated plaid pricked at my thighs through the sticky wet of my cotton slip. It was my job to heat up the O'Keefe and Merritt double pancake griddle until it was spit-hissing hot and turn the hot flat bread when she finished rolling it.

Clack, clack, turn. Mother talked and rolled out more flat bread.

"Get a move on there!" Mother hollered back to me between clacks and slaps.

The big mound of flour tortilla dough had to be ready before she got up the hill from the number 47 bus, the last of her two buses home from the envelope factory. Big, round, and smeared with lard to keep it from drying, it had to be ready so she could break it up into hand-sized mounds and roll them out.

Her purse and lunch bag on the matching yellow vinyl chair by the yellow Formica, she rolled the dough out faster than I could turn it two at a time on the double pancake griddle. Once the rolling really got going, the clacks and slaps made a rhythm that took her far away from where she was, to where she sometimes went, rolling and remembering back to Utah.

"When my little brother Sal died, they put him in the living room. There were little lights all around his head. I can still see those lights. White candles burned down to nothing all around his head," she said.

Clack, clack, turn. Mother talked and rolled, and I cooked on the stove behind her. I was there but not there.

Until I could lay it on the griddle, the rolled round bread hung everywhere, on the backs of torn yellow vinyl chairs away from the exposed gray cotton stuffing, on top of the faded tin blue flower bread box, on the windowsill with the rusted screen behind it, and all around the rippled chromed edge of the kitchen table.

Clack, clack, turn.

"There was a party at the house the day my brother died. It

was a baptism. Everybody was there. All your uncles and all the Utah relations were there. We were playing outside," she said.

Clack, clack, turn.

The round dough cooked bubbles into the middle of the bread. My fingers scorched every time I tried to turn the half-cooked flat bread with my hands. After each finger-burning turn, I dug my swollen hands in the red wool of my skirt and held them between my legs. When that didn't work, I put my fingers in my mouth. On the worst days when I was sure she wasn't looking, I took a fork to the bread, stabbed it, and flipped it over like a pancake. That worked until one of my brothers wanted to know about the four evenly spaced puncture marks on the side of the bread.

"How come there's holes in the tortillas?" Ted asked.

Mother's broomstick rolling pin rolled up and around in a wide radius between clacks and slaps and slammed flat on the back of my hand, pushing my fingers into the hot and shiny scratched silver griddle.

"Use your hands, goddamn it. How many times have I told you to use your goddamn hands? How are you ever going to find a husband?" Mother said.

Proper Utah-born Mexican women used their hands; only Eastside slackers like me used a fork. I held my limp, burnt hands between my legs in the red plaid pleats of my skirt. I was doomed to be a spinster.

Clack, clack, turn. The more Mother rolled, the more she remembered, and the more she could tell her stories like she could tell them without telling them at all.

"His padrino ran 'im over. That's how Sal died. He got run over. Right after the *bolo*. The *bolo* is the old custom where they throw the money out for kids to run after when they baptize a baby," she explained.

Clack, clack, turn.

Mother's telling trance rolled on with the flat bread.

"We had just got back from the church. The old Lady of Guadalupe Church where you were baptized in Salt Lake. The baptized baby's padrino threw the change out like candy from a broke piñata. There were quarters, dimes, nickels, pennies. Somebody said there was a silver dollar," she said.

Mother stopped just long enough to peel more cracked dough off her fingers and rubbed her hands against her thighs into her pinned-on kitchen dirt apron over her Tuesday dress, the blue paisley, her favorite. More bread—*clack, clack, turn.*

"We ran after the money and put it in our socks. The pennies went under the car," she said.

She pushed and pulled harder against the table in a rhythm and roll that seemed to lift her out of where she was, away from us, our kitchen, our house, our neighborhood. Back to Utah. Back to the Wasatch Mountains, the Great Salt Lake, Pioneer Park, the Founder's Day Parade, Saltair, the Terrace Ballroom, The Cinco "R's" on Second South, "El Abandonado," and yam pies at Thanksgiving.

Clack, clack, turn. The mounds of dough were almost all rolled out.

"The pennies went under his padrino's car. Sal went after them," she said.

The dough from Mother's apron caked off as she rolled and talked, and it fell into dried bits around her feet. The black heels under her weight made dent marks in the yellow linoleum where she stood, leaned, and worked enough flour dough into tortillas to feed eleven of us.

Clack, clack, turn.

"He went after those pennies," she said.

She bent into the table and rolled out the last dozen.

"His padrino rolled the car out, and Sal got stuck under the tire. The car went into reverse, and Sal couldn't get out," she said.

Clack, clack, turn.

"His head got smashed," she said.

The round bread on the griddle bubbled up like a blowfish when it cooked on both sides. Cooked hot bread in my hands, I bounced the flour balloon on my burnt fingers in three steps to the kitchen table into a fresh dishcloth laid open in a basket. I took a sideways look at her to see her eyes rolled up to the sky outside our kitchen window.

Clack, clack, turn.

"I was supposed to be watching him," she said.

Clack, clack, turn.

"I was supposed to be taking care of him. Your grandma Mary cried and cried and almost went crazy when my brother Sal died," she said.

My fingers in my mouth, there were burn holes in the bread when I got back to it.

"I was supposed to be watching him," she repeated.

The second dead baby. Doroteo Rico.

Clack, clack, turn.

"They threw your great-grandma Mercedes in jail with her son Doroteo for hiding your great-grandpa Cirilo," Mother said. "That's how that baby died. Doroteo Rico died when he got sick in there in the jail with your great-grandma Mercedes," she said.

Clack, clack, turn.

My cousin, Doroteo Lawson, or D, as he came to be known, was born to my aunt Estella and uncle Gerald in the late 1950s. His dad, my uncle Gerald, was a descendant of the five families who came to Utah as Mormon slaves. Uncle Gerald and Aunt Estella, my mother's sister, fell in love at the Utah State Youth Detention Center, where they were put for whatever youths of color were rounded up for in 1950s Utah. When they got out, Uncle Gerald came to the steps of our house on South West Temple to visit Aunt Estella while my parents were at work. He wasn't supposed to be there. The grandmas, Mary and Mercedes, sent Aunt Estella to us to be our babysitter when Aunt Estella got out of the detention center and couldn't go back to school because she was pregnant.

In a white T-shirt over cuffed jeans, James Dean–style, Uncle Gerald was sixteen, and Aunt Estella was fourteen. Even though none of us could see his generations of Lawsons, they were all there on the porch with Uncle Gerald. Invisible, but standing in the lives and stories of survival.

Aunt Estella snuck him in. I saw my aunt and uncle through the crack in the door to my parents' bedroom. He with his generations of Lawsons held her and her three generations of Utah Mexicans. In her white pedal pushers and a sleeveless red-checked gingham blouse, she stood at the edge of Mother's pink-and-green chenille bedspread. The veins in Uncle Gerald's arms bulged against her gingham back. With his other hand on the side of her face, he pushed her white headband back and ran his tongue along her lips. He pulled her to the door and shut it with his back blocking our view.

When their son, my cousin D, was born, the state of Utah took him away because Aunt Estella was underage.

"*Que se lo llevan*," my great-grandma Mercedes had said. *They can take him.*

Neither she nor Grandma Mary wanted Black people in our family.

When they took him away, Aunt Estella turned herself inside out and told Great-Grandma Mercedes and Grandma Mary, "You better get my baby back."

Nobody in my family ever talked to them like that. Aunt Estella saying "you better" was talking so crazy to them, little and sick as she was, just the force of her saying it moved them off her bed.

In my family, saying "you better" meant doing what our outlaw patriarch did. It meant being willing to stand up to a posse of ninety men and drawing your weapon, knowing you were going to die and still declaring your love.

12

Mercedes and Mary brought cousin D home because they really didn't want to know. Because they already knew. Because Aunt Estella found it in her somewhere to summon our first patriarch, Cirilo Rico.

Cirilo Rico, who, on the way to getting killed, after escaping from jail, after killing the Mormon deputy they sent after him, after stopping a Mormon family in a wagon and letting them go, said, "I have a family too," as reported in the *Salt Lake Tribune*, just before he was shot by a posse of ninety men in Utah in October of 1922.

It was a sign to Mercedes and Mary that, Black or not, cousin D was ours. No Mormon protective agency would get him. He was ours.

My beatnik-cum-hippie uncle said Mercedes was "down" with cousin D after that. That's why they named him Doroteo. Cirilo Rico had sent her back her dead son.

Clack, clack, turn.

The third dead baby, Cirila Rico.

There was no card, flower, favorite food, picture, or story in the shrine for the dead babies for Cirila Rico, but I knew she was there. I knew it every time I was fed, bathed, clothed, and put to bed at Mercedes's house. I knew it when I sat in my specially upholstered, child-sized chair. When I put on my Mickey Mouse ears to watch the *Mickey Mouse Club* on our Philco TV. When I played in Great-Grandma's garden and marveled at spiders and webs for hours on end. When I went to get candy from the corner drugstore and could put it on my very own tab. When I swung on my swing and my great-grandpa Vidal climbed to the very top of the cherry tree to bring me bowls full of cherries.

As a child in Mercedes's world, there were purple-and-red-painted, metal twirling toys, sugar breads shaped into shells, bride dolls, long flats of freshly rendered *chicharrones*, flat brown shiny piggy cookies, delicately spiced rice, and brush-painted rodeo dresses with sequined ponies and lariats on them.

I knew these things long before I knew the pink against brown of my own mother's cheeks and the cavity in the middle of her teeth. My mother, who at seventeen had fallen in love with an itinerant medical student from Mexico City, conceived me after a Founder's Day dance, and gave me to Mercedes to raise.

Clack, clack, turn.

"When you were a baby," Mother said, "the only way you would sleep was with *canela* mixed in your milk. Your great-grandma Mercedes was so afraid that you might die that she called the doctor every time you got sick."

Clack, clack, turn.

"She called so much, even when you weren't sick, he told her to give you *canela*, cinnamon stick with your milk," she said.

My bed at Mercedes's house was painted pink and had wooden rails on the sides of it. It's the only bed I remember from my childhood. The day the doctor came, my nose was stuffed and my throat hurt so bad I couldn't cry. I turned back and forth, twisted up in my wet nightgown and the bedsheets with my head against the bedrails.

The doctor came in with his black suit and bag. Great-Grandma walked over to him with a wrung-out white hanky in her hands. Leaving his black bag by the door, the doctor walked over to my bed. Great-Grandma untangled me and pushed back the snot-dried hair that was stuck to my red-hot swollen face. The doctor lifted my shirt, put his cold tool on my heart, touched my head, and opened my mouth with a stick.

Great-Grandma took her money out of her dress, where she kept it rolled up next to her heart. She took the rolled-up money and put it on the table under the hearth shrine to the dead babies.

Her red flower print dress pushed through the bedrail slats where she stood over me opposite the doctor. He held a spoon above me. I knocked it out of his hand and rolled over to cover my face.

Great-Grandma rolled me back and looked at the doctor, like it was all her fault. Like she'd better do something, or he might leave. Her face red with tears, she put her hands on my shoulders and held me down. The doctor poured out another spoonful and landed the pink liquid in my mouth. I spat it out.

This time, reaching so that the entire top of her red flowered dress was over my bedrail, Mercedes grabbed my throat, closed my nose, and opened my mouth. I cried and gagged so hard I couldn't make a sound. The thick, sweet pink liquid ran down my throat, and some of the cold pink slid down my cheek, down my neck.

Back in the kitchen with mother, my memory was interrupted by the steady *clack, clack* roll of her hand in the dough on the yellow Formica.

Clack, clack, turn.

"Your great-grandma Mercedes hid your great-grandpa Cirilo Rico under a tarp when he escaped from jail. He killed the deputy who they sent to find him in a shoot-out. They knew the law was coming after him, so that night he told your great-grandma Mercedes, 'Don't look for me or come after me when I leave tonight. Just look for my hat.'"

Because there were never stories, pictures, or a name for Cirila Rico, not like the other dead babies, I only found her in my decades-long search of State of Utah Vital Statistics records for the death certificate of Cirilo Rico, her father, our first patriarch, the notorious Millard Bandit. After several attempts that twice yielded a half sheet form letter that said they had no record of his death, I called the State of Utah Vital Statistics Bureau.

"I don't have a Cirilo Rico," a kindly state archives worker told me over the phone when I spoke to her from my then-office in Portland, Oregon.

"How can there be no record of his death?" I said. "The account of his killing is on the front page of the *Salt Lake Tribune* and the *Deseret News* in October 1922."

"Sorry, hon, don't have a Cirilo, but I do have a Cirila Rico, who died around the same time," she said.

Cirila Rico died when she was a year old in a boardinghouse in Highland Boy, Utah, in 1923. Named for her father, her birth certificate showed the cause of death to be bronchial pneumonia. She was born five months after a Utah posse killed her father, my great-grandfather Cirilo Rico, the so-called Millard Bandit, and thirty years before I was born.

It was the cause of her death, and the absence of any visible remembrance of her in any of the dead baby shrines or the family stories, that brought her alive to me. She was the namesake of the man who had thrown his hat into the air as a gesture of love to Mercedes when the posse circled him for the kill.

As she told it, it was an act of love for her, not a surrender.

This is how I discovered the existence of Cirila Rico, the third dead baby that nobody in my family knew about except Mercedes.

"Would you like us to send her to you?" the archives worker on the phone asked.

"Yes, please send her to me," I replied.

When Cirila Rico's death certificate arrived, I knew I'd found the missing piece of Mercedes's shrine.

CHAPTER 3

CHICKEN FRIED RICE

I was six years old and waited by the window for Mother, who at that time was almost as unknown to me as my grandma Mary was. We were still living in Salt Lake when Mother came to pick me up to visit Mary.

My big button, white collar, Little Orphan Annie coat covered me to my knees. I wore white lace-trimmed anklets and black patent leather shoes. My feet hung just over the edge of the overstuffed sofa by the big window at my great-grandma Mercedes's house, where I lived with her and Great-Grandpa Vidal. They were the only parents I knew.

Mother's black drawstring purse bounced against the leather sides of her jacket when she walked up the steps. She sometimes came by to take me shopping or to the park to play with my brothers. She lifted me up to her, and I made a circle with my arms around her neck. My face in the sweet leather smell of her collar, my stomach curved around her breasts, she carried me downstairs to the idling Hudson. I sat in the front seat on white stitched leather between Mother and her husband.

My brothers tumbled over each other in the back seat on our way to Mary's. The green Hudson rolled over the snow like it was carpet under the State Street archway.

Mary lived on Second South in rooms on top of a row of storefronts where our family had owned a succession of Salt Lake City Mexican restaurants since the 1930s. We had places with names like "Los Cinco 'R's" and "El Abandonado."

Mother carried me up the stairs to a six-panel door that had three locks on it and a hole where the doorknob used to be. In her arms, Mother made a swing for me. I rested myself against her and sat in her laced hands like the song she sang.

"Would you like to swing on a star?" Mother sang.

Mother's face was cream colored, like the cream in my great-grandpa's coffee just poured.

"Carry moonbeams home in a jar?" Mother sang.

Her lips were pink like the painted pink top of Mexican coconut candy, the kind behind glass in Great-Grandma's restaurant.

"Or would you rather be a mule?" Mother sang.

In 1950s Utah, the candy, *pan dulce*, Cantinflas puppets, and sequined rodeo dresses came in boxes big enough for me to climb into. Like everything else we needed to be Mexican in Utah, they came by rail up from Central Mexico, from cities unknown to me, to the Mexican side of Salt Lake City where we lived, and where we ran businesses other than the restaurant, businesses that the Mormons patronized but couldn't own.

Mother's red nails hit the door.

"A-tisket, a-tasket, I lost my yellow basket . . ." Mother sang.

The door opened to windows with sheets pulled back to show the brick wall of another building. In rooms that smelled of *comino*, roasted and sweated ancho chiles, the sticky grit of barbacoa, and roasted calf heads, two women and two men sat around a coffee table that had burn holes all around it. Behind them, there was a scratched, painted-brown metal bed with sheets and blankets spilled down around it on the scarred plank floor.

The unmatched, scratched, yellow, red, and blue wooden chairs teetered like my kindergarten chairs. Two couples sat in a circle around the cigarette-burned coffee table that held Grandma's golden ashtray in the middle of it.

Pink against red, Mother's lips met Grandma's.

Mother bent over to hand me to Grandma. Her purse at her back, me in her arms, Mother made a bent-kneed scoot closer to Grandma. She rested her elbow against Grandma's blue peg-legged chair. Mother tipped me into Grandma. I bunched up tighter around Mother's neck, my backside on Grandma's lap. Mother's lips pressed together, pink to pink.

Grandma lifted a burning cigarette from her golden ashtray. She inhaled and printed the pattern of her lips on the cigarette, then exhaled. Grandma's eyelids were flat, and you could only see the red in her eyes. In her rooms, Grandma only wore satin. Grandma smoothed the white satin skirt on her lap. Mother broke the curve of my body against hers. I could only see Mother's chipped front tooth behind the opening and closing of her pink lips.

"I'll come back to get you later," Mother said. "Like we talked about, remember?"

Grandma's man, Mr. Sanchez, wore a thick black brush of a mustache and wavy, neat-cut, salt-and-pepper hair. We only knew his last name. That was all we needed to know. "You can change a man," Mary liked to say, "like a man changes his shirt, and sometimes his shirts will fit the new man." The starched flannel sleeve of Mr. Sanchez's shirt covered his arm to his wrist.

"Come on, little girl," he said in a Texan drawl.

He took a pack of cigarettes out of his creased shirt pocket. "I won't bite," he said.

A crease line ran up and down the brown plaid patch of his shirt pocket. Grandma pulled the narrow strap of her satin slip up over her shoulder.

"That's 'cause you ain't got no teeth," Grandma said.

The other man who sat around the table spat out his beer when he laughed. Grandma flicked her ashes into the golden ashtray and extended her cigarette to him.

"This is Chief," she said.

Chief had long black hair tied behind his head and wore a shirt with a collar that stood stiff, like it had been ironed and the rest of the shirt hadn't. Grandma pulled in to inhale and blew her smoke in the direction of, but turned her head away from, the woman next to him.

"And this is Chiefa, his wife," she said.

Chief tapped his near-empty beer can on the cigarette table burns, and Chiefa got up to get him another beer. He took the last swig of his beer and folded his can with one hand.

"What's the matter? Don't you want to stay and visit with your grandma?" Chief asked.

Mr. Sanchez took a drag of his cigarette. "Watch," he said.

His cheeks opened and closed. His mustache even and flat against his lips, he leaned forward and blew out a white circle of smoke. The smoke hung in the air, and then, like a ghost, it changed shape.

Mother pulled my arms away from her neck and closed them on my lap. Under me, Grandma's lap was warm, leg to lap, only her satin slip between us. A white circle floated by.

"Come on, sit with your grandma and I'll make you another one," Mr. Sanchez said.

A large smoke ring floated and landed like a halo around Grandma's head. I reached for the smoke ring, touched it, and it disappeared.

There was gold in Grandma's mouth when she laughed, gold from during the war, from when she was making good money. Where her *comadres* had embedded diamonds in their teeth, Grandma preferred gold. When she was making good money, she sent her kids their dinner home in a cab. Even as an adult, Mother associated Peking duck and chicken fried rice with yellow cabs.

Mother's black capri pants crisscrossed like scissors over to the brick framed window. Her silhouette against the building across the street, she stood sideways to get a view of the street. She opened her purse and pulled out her lipstick and mirror.

"Tony and the kids are waiting for me downstairs," Mother said.

Mother pulled her purse shut and slung it around her back.

"Mom, I've gotta go," Mother said.

The side slits of Mother's capris opened over her calves when she bent over to kiss me.

"You're gonna stay for a visit with your grandma, okay?" Mother said.

I reached for Mother's neck and pulled myself around her to find that sweet leather smell.

Chief slid his beer to Grandma.

"Don't you wanna stay and visit some more?" Chief said.

I felt the satin of Grandma's slip between my legs and in the back of my thighs. I shook my head and looked back at Grandma's gold against the red of her lips when she smiled.

"I've gotta take her, Mom. She doesn't want to stay," Mother said.

Grandma's satin slip moved up her thigh when Mother lifted me off Grandma's lap. Grandma smoothed down her satin over her lap and reached for her cigarette.

CHAPTER 4

THE DIFFERENCE BETWEEN A WHORE AND A WORKING WOMAN

It was one of those Salt Lake winters, when the snow was so fat that it knocked on the door to see if we wanted to play. By then, I was living in a two-story Craftsman on South West Temple with Mother, my stepfather, and six of my seven brothers. The black phone rang fire-alarm loud for Mother.

"You'd better come and get Mary," the caller said.

"She's shut Frank's down again," Mother said.

Before Mother could dispatch Stepdad to the tavern, a yellow cab pulled up at the end of our walkway.

The newest baby was in his crib, near enough to the fireplace to keep warm but not get burned. The rest of us were on the couch under a green army blanket with our backs to the window. We sat together with three panels of snow as our backdrop. Looking out the side window, we could see exclamation points cut by Grandma's tiny heels in the new snow on the cleared sidewalk past the big balls of snow we'd rolled the day before for that day's snowman.

Grandma Mary pushed open our chain-link gate, leaving it wide open. She was up our red steps like a life-size, spark-spitting top, her black swing coat in a full circle around her.

Mother opened the front door to a rush of cold, snow, and Grandma. Her black heels clicked across the black-and-white foyer. Mother tried to slide open the pocket door to let her in to the living room, but it got stuck mid-pull. I took another glance out the window and could see Grandma's smashed cigarette in the snow outside.

"Goddamn sons of bitches," Mary said. "Pinche Frank tried to cut us out again."

Mother pulled hard to unstick the pocket door and slid it closed crooked behind Grandma. Hairpins fell out of Grandma's hair onto her fur collar. She turned the top rhinestone-studded button on her black wool coat.

"We cost him more today than he'll make in a week, cabrón," she said. "*Hijo de la chingada.*"

Son of a bitch.

Grandma's lipstick was gone. She walked over to the fire-place, pulled one arm out of her coat, and kicked the caked snow off her black heels into the fire. We stared at her from under our barricade of blankets. She caught us and took a step toward us.

"What the hell are you all looking at?" she said. "This ain't no goddamn bingo game," she added.

We hunched deeper into the couch. She pulled her other arm out of her coat.

Mother took her coat and picked the baby bottle up from the chair by the fire and pointed it to us and to the pocket door.

"You kids get upstairs," Mother instructed.

We'd learned to walk in one line like a centipede, with the littlest brother in front. We moved into formation in bare feet over our blanket. Mother laid Grandma's coat on the chair by the fire where she had been feeding the baby.

Grandma bent over and lit a cigarette from the fireplace.

"Get me a beer, will you, Margaret?" Grandma said.

Grandma walked back and forth in front of the fireplace while we lined up to leave, her black heels on the inlaid tiles. Beer in hand, she sat down and balanced her cigarette in a Skippy peanut butter jar lid on the chair arm. I moved the centipede of kids through the pocket door to the foyer and tried to close it all the way.

"Come here," Grandma said.

My brothers were almost up the stairs. My feet on the warm hardwood wouldn't move.

"Come on," she said. "Come see your grandma for a minute."

I walked over to her by the fire.

"Let 'er go, Mom," Mother said, folding the baby tighter in his blanket.

I stood before Grandma with my back to the fire. She pushed my hair back and put her hand on my face.

"Someday, mija," she said. "Someday, you'll learn the difference between a whore and a working woman."

Mother smacked the baby bottle down on the mantel above the fire.

"You get upstairs now," Mother told me.

I went back to the pocket door and tried to pull it shut behind me. Mother shook the baby bottle at me.

"And don't come back down until I call you!"

Grandma pulled the tab off her beer, took a sip, and leaned into the fire.

"I cut my own goddamn deals. Every girl in there does. Frank gets his cut on the drinks. That's all he gets," she said.

She took a sip of her beer.

"Son of a bitch," she said.

The pocket door wouldn't budge.

"Frank's been trying to run the trade in there again, and some of those bitches were just giving it away," Grandma said.

With her back to the fire, Mother propped the baby bottle up with a rolled-up blanket to the baby's mouth in the bassinet.

"I told you to get upstairs," Mother repeated.

I ran across the foyer, my feet against the cold black-and-white tiles and the melted snow that Grandma tracked in.

"Leave 'er alone, Margaret," Grandma said.

Before Mother could get the pocket door completely closed, I heard my grandma begin to cry.

"I know I haven't been a good mother to you, Margaret," Grandma said.

"It's alright, Mom," Mother replied.

"I know you deserved better," Grandma said.

"Just take it easy, Mom," Mother said. "Just take it easy."

I became a union official, organizing strikes and huge public citywide protest actions. It's easy to see that I learned early lessons about leverage from Mary. That sometimes you need to break things up to make your point.

And I can only wonder how many times my granny's hooker code about the difference between being a whore and a working woman led me through the many times I could have sold myself out but didn't. Walking the line, doing what was right, no matter the cost.

CHAPTER 5

UNCLE JERRY

Our house in Salt Lake, the big Craftsman on South West Temple, didn't have a backyard. It had a warehouse built over the back of it. There were large square wooden walls that closed off the alley and huge swing-open doors made of dark weather-stained wood. There was dirt, rocks, and broken glass everywhere. It smelled of mildew and oil. There was no back porch, only a loading dock. We played in the dark, under the platform in the back of the warehouse.

When I was seven and Uncle Jerry was eleven, he came to live with us. He had been sent away from where he had been living for "doing bad things." He would come into my room when he thought I was asleep. My bed was by the door where I could see the alcove window that looked like a little altar. The window was right by the tree where I could keep my eye out for Bloody Bones. The tree held soft snow even when it was naked in the winter and spread big giant green leaves like sheets next to the wooden frame of our house in the summer. I'd pretend to be asleep when he lifted my nightie to touch me.

Other times he would come up to my room and put toys around the room, a ball, a doll, or other toys. He'd pick up a toy and ask me if I wanted it. I'd stand by my alcove window with my back to it, and he'd stand on the other side of the room by the built-in dresser with the missing drawers near the door so I couldn't get out.

"Come get the ball," he'd say.

I'd run to the ball, and he'd grab me in places where he touched me in the night when I pretended to be asleep. There were toys in the room that I wanted and could only have if I let him touch me.

One day I went upstairs after school and waited for my grandma Mary, Uncle Jerry's mother, at the top of the stairs outside of my bedroom. The stairs were wooden and had carved spindles on the sides of them to keep you from falling over the railing. I waited and wore the dress she'd made for me. It was a lavender dotted Swiss with a full gathered skirt and lace collar. I wore my Easter Sunday white patent leather shoes and white lace anklets.

Grandma came up the stairs with a basket of sheets on her hip to change the sheets on the beds and to sweep the landing outside our bedrooms. Grandma's black hair was rolled up around her head in a scarf. The red roses on the scarf matched her apron.

She passed me on the step, so I followed her to the landing. There were two windows on the landing and a bench next to the window where I read my Baltimore Catechism to prepare for my First Communion. I read about Jesus being God's only begotten son, God's beloved son. *What is a beloved son? What is begotten?* I wondered.

Grandma went to sit on the bench under the window. My ink-blue catechism was there under the window, open to the question page. She put her basket of sheets down next to her, and the only thing between us on the bench was the light that shined through the window. Grandma smoothed her hands under the hem of my skirt over the stiches she made.

"Grandma," I said. "Uncle Jerry."

I wanted to say it first so I could get it out and not be afraid to tell her. Grandma dropped my hem and pulled the basket of sheets onto her lap.

"What about Uncle Jerry?" she asked.

Grandma tightened her hands around the white woven reed handles of the basket. The clean sheets stuck out over the sides of the wicker basket, and Grandma stuffed them back in.

"Uncle Jerry's been coming into my room," I said.

She pushed a stray hair under her head scarf and lifted herself and the basket of sheets in front of her.

"Don't tell me," she said. She shifted the sheet basket to her hip and walked back to the stairs. "Tell your mother," she instructed.

I stood over the spindle railing at the top of the landing with my catechism in my hand and watched Grandma turn at the bottom of the stairs with the white wicker basket balanced on her hips. The roses on her scarf turned the corner with her and left.

Telling my mother was like giving my mother a belt and asking her to beat me with it. In Mother's world, anything that happened to you was your fault. Still, I waited by my bedroom door at the top of the landing for Mother to come home from her late-night laundry shift when everyone was asleep. Night after night I waited for her, but even though I could hear her steps, I couldn't make myself call out to her. Each night I waited, believing that telling her would be worse than what was happening to me.

The grocer at the corner store wore a blue wraparound apron that tied in the front. The back wrapped all around his waist and tied in the front into a lazy one-loop bow. The blue apron had a pocket holder on the front where he kept his pens. He handed me a brown paper bag with a quart of milk for our snack and a can of tomato sauce for the rice.

"Is that all for you today?" he asked.

He counted out the change and pressed the dime, nickel, and penny into my hand.

I moved my head to say yes. I never said any words to the grocery man. On the way out the door, I walked by the pencils and things for writing that I liked: the click pens, the markers, and the steno pads. I really liked the pastel-greenish pages of the steno pads, their hard, cardboard covers, even blue lines, and the red stripe right down the middle. When he wasn't looking, I grabbed a handful of pencils and threw them into my bag. I closed my brown paper bag and gripped it, crushing the paper in my fist. I had to have something that was mine, clean, crisp, and new; even though I had been beaten when Mother thought I took a Hoppy Taw, I didn't care. I had to have them.

I walked to the light and pushed the button. I waited for the cars to stop and walked home past the house where the Mormon kids lived and by the house where the kids who threw rocks at us lived. Nobody lived in the house right next to our house. It had no back door and no windows. I took my pencils out of my sack and threw them in the bush in the empty lot right outside my window.

I couldn't bring the pencils in the house, and I needed to have them close by. I needed them to be shiny and new. I needed them to have smooth edges, to be unsharpened and flat at the end so I could see the lead, and they needed to have full erasers. I needed them to say the words new pencils say on them: *no. 2, Ticonderoga, Nathan Hale.*

One day on my way home from school, I stopped by the bush in the empty lot to find my pencils.

"Where are you going?" Grandma Mary called to me from the front door. She came out to the porch and rubbed her hands in the skirt of her apron.

"This is your house," she said. "Why are you going over there?"

I opened the gate and walked up the red stairs. Grandma waited for me in the red flowered apron she always wore. The red roses of her apron skirt were wrinkled up in her hands.

Telling her about the pencils was like telling her about Uncle Jerry, something she didn't want to know about, because if she didn't know about it, it didn't happen. The pencils were mine, something she didn't know about, so therefore they didn't happen.

Later I found my pencils in the bush in the empty lot where the haunted house was and brought them into the house and put them in my drawer next to my Easter anklets, pink rosary, and First Communion veil.

The next time I went to the store, the grocer in the blue apron put the money in my hand, closed the register, walked around the counter, put his hands on my elbows, and walked me to the door.

"I think your mother is going to need that milk soon," he said.

I almost never went to the pencils alone after that. When he could, the grocer always stood by and watched me so that I couldn't grab the pencils anymore, so that I couldn't touch the rubber tips of clean erasers. To this day, I still hoard pencils with clean erasers.

Many years later, I returned to Salt Lake for a family reunion. I told one of my uncles what Uncle Jerry had done to me as a child and that I did not feel comfortable being around him.

He called Uncle Jerry and told him that he was not welcome to the picnic because of what I had said. Jerry cried on the phone, said he was sorry, and hung up. All these years later, when I reflect on the pattern of abuse that Jerry as an eleven-year-old boy did to me, and what I came to subsequently learn about what happened to Mary, I can only conclude that it was learned and that he was mimicking what had been done to him. Had it happened to others in my family? To my mother? Is that why she liked the Jane Wyman movie *Johnny Belinda* so much, and why she named my sister Belinda? Is that why she could not protect me?

I never had the opportunity to talk to Jerry about it; he died not long after.

CHAPTER 6

WONDER BREAD

To notice my brother's whiteness would have been to notice Mother's black eyes, her swollen face, and the scratch marks on my stepfather's back. To notice would have been to notice my stepfather beating my mother when he got drunk or when he was sober, just to show his in-laws that he could.

To notice would have been to find out how Sal got to be in the middle of the nine of us, a white kid in the middle of nine Mexicans, all Stepdad's kids but me, the eldest, and Sal, the middle of seven sons.

To notice would have been to learn that Mother had tried to find another husband when Stepdad got deported, that her father, my grandpa Vidal, had called the INS on Stepdad to stop him from beating Mother. That during my stepdad's deportation, my mother and her sisters tried to find her another husband. How when finding another husband didn't work, Mother ended up with a baby from a white man. She had to keep the baby, us being Catholic and all. To notice would have been to ask if the guy was Mormon. Being white was one thing; being Mormon was another. There were lots of white Catholics. Being Catholic in Mormon Utah had its own community of customs, conformities, bonds, and ethics. In some ways, marrying outside your faith was worse than marrying outside your race, unless you married a Black man in 1950s Utah.

On the other hand, to notice would have helped me understand why Mother was always suspicious of any white man I knew, especially of my white second husband. Where Stepdad as an immigrant Mexican worker railed at blatant Mormon bigotry, would get into fights in bars and get thrown out into the street, Mother's aversion was so subversive, I don't think even she saw it.

Opening the door just a crack to Sal's whiteness would have opened the door to more than we as children could ever see or know about our parents. Doors that opened beyond Mother's swollen face and black eyes and my brother's white skin. Doors that opened to all the family stories and secrets, to what happened to the dead babies and to what my family did to survive the Depression in 1930s Utah, doors that were closed back-to-back, story after story, year after year, Utah to LA and back, to the many things we knew were there but couldn't see.

I heard a version of Stepdad's deportation as an adult in a car ride with my parents and then-husband on a trip to Mexico from LA. This trip was one of my few visits back home to LA.

We moved from Utah to LA when I was eight. Mother had successfully sued Great-Grandma Mercedes for custody of me. Stepdad got the Union Pacific to transfer him out of Salt Lake so he could get away from my mother's family, the Mormons, and from all that went with being a Mexican immigrant in 1950s Utah.

My husband had just gotten his new used top-of-the-line Toyota, and Stepdad wanted to show us the Tijuana of his youth.

My parents sat next to each other in the back seat, and the telling of it began when Stepdad "started something." Starting something usually meant Stepdad saying something Mother didn't want to hear, usually something anti-American. Mother was a solid Utahan; she believed in the stars and stripes, Uncle Sam, and all that it meant to be a patriotic American. Stepdad's politics were more to the left. He grew up during the presidency of Lázaro Cárdenas, when the oil companies were nationalized and priests were forbidden to wear religious clothing in public.

Almost as soon as we got on the south-bound Santa Ana Freeway, my stepdad's hand pulled back on the inside of the front passenger seat, where I sat next to my husband. Both of Stepdad's hands pulled my seat hard enough to turn me back to face him in the space between my seat and my husband's. Mother's head was turned to the car door window behind my husband's seat, her hands folded on her lap. Stepdad squinted a look back at Mother like he was about to try to get away with something, something that was worth getting in trouble for. Like he had waited a long time to tell somebody who would listen. He looked back at Mother once more.

"You grandpa Vidal, he call de Migra on me," he said close enough to my ear that even whispered, everyone could hear it. Mother went deep into her Utah dialect when she got disgusted, into a nasally drawl with her vowels stretched out to make a point.

"Tony, my family had nothing to do with that," she said.

"Yes, dey do," he said. "When I was in de office, de migrante, he say dey no was lookin' for nobody en de [railroad] track dat day. 'You wife family,' he say. 'They call it.'"

Mother took her hanky, folded it, refolded it, and smoothed it down on her lap. She directed her voice out the window. "That's not true," she replied.

Stepdad pulled my seat again to be sure I was listening. "He say dey no was lookin' for nobody. Dey no gonna wais' time yus for one Mexican," Stepdad continued.

"No, they didn't," Mother said.

"Dey do," Stepdad said. "How dey know where was I dat day? En de track?" he asked. "Good God, Tony, I don't know," Mother said.

He pulled my seat again and pushed his face between the front passenger and driver seats; this time we were just a nose away from each other. "Because you grampa, he de only one who know where was I dat day."

"Like I said, my family had nothing to do with it," Mother insisted.

Stepdad turned his head only far enough to send words partway back to Mother. "Who gonna tell it?"

"Like I said, I don't know," Mother replied.

"He de only one who know," Stepdad said.

"Good grief, Tony," she said.

Both of Stepdad's eyes stared at me in the rearview mirror. "You grampa Vidal, he de only one, he de only one who know," Stepdad said.

Mother did a full turn away from us.

"Like I said, Tony, my family had nothing to do with it," she repeated.

Their dispute continued all the way to Mexico and back and for the rest of their married lives. It was never resolved, and it never would be. But now at least there was a disputed version about something that nobody talked about.

By itself, to notice a white kid in the middle of nine Mexicans would have been to hold a story too big for children to manage, a narrative too heavy for us to carry. Yet its heaviness weighed on us. It was all around in everything that everybody who knew us saw but acted like they didn't see. And even if they pretended not to know, it was in the unspoken words that everybody who knew us knew about us but didn't say. And in knowing what they knew, they knew us in ways we didn't know ourselves.

Still, there were clues about Sal. Clues hidden in plain sight, like in his very naming. First off, Mother named him, not Stepdad.

Stepdad's naming of his six sons resulted in multisyllabic vowel-laden first and middle names that rang like poetry when spoken in Spanish. My name and Sal's were short or unpronounceable in Spanish.

Secondly, Stepdad named one of my brothers after a revered Mexican movie star and another after a beloved uncle. Mother named Sal after a dead baby. A dead little boy she was supposed to be taking care of when he died. I was named after a nurse who was kind to Mother at a segregated hospital where I was born, Mormon (white) on one side, Catholic (Mexican) on another.

Then there were the Grandma Jenny rations. Grandma Jenny was Stepdad's mother. She came to run the household when Mother went back to work between having babies. When Jenny served our food, Sal got the smallest bowl, even when he wasn't the youngest. His piece of meat was measured against his younger brother's portion and was always smaller. When we got the rice milk frozen treats she made for us, Sal got no spoon. At dinnertime, he was put in a high chair away from the table and left to make a mess. Any time she could, she shorted him his food, giving him the burnt tortilla, the bruised banana, and the leftover rice.

The odd thing about Jenny was that she was blonde and blue-eyed from the part of Mexico in Mazatlán where the French soldiers quartered under Maximilian. Her contempt for Sal's whiteness was not a lack of solidarity with whiteness but more her unwillingness to let go of Mother's betrayal. Jenny kept score, even if her son, my stepdad, didn't.

When Stepdad made his way back to Salt Lake after his deportation, Mother's belly had a cloth circle cut around it in the skirt she wore under her maternity smock. The string that brought up the sides of curved fabric cut to fit around her belly tied into a neat bow on top. He found her at a restaurant much like the one he met her in. The music on the tabletop jukebox was a combination of Mexican trio music like Los Tres Ases with songs like

"No Me Platiques Ya" and "Venganza" on one side, three songs for a quarter, and Patsy Cline's "Crazy," Johnny Ray's "Cry," and Frankie Lane on the other. That's how they talked to each other from completely opposite sides of the language spectrum.

Years later, when Mother was gone and my marriage ended, I visited with Stepdad and asked him why he came back to her when he knew her baby wasn't his.

"*Me senti como huerfano sin ella*," he said about why he came back. *I felt like an orphan without her.*

"When I came back, jue mader, chee tell me, 'Jue free to go, Tony. I double-cross jue. Jue have no obligation to me no more. I double-cross jue. Jue free to go,'" he said.

It sounded right to me, what he said Mother said and how she said it. It was in that Utah way about doing "huat's riiight" with "i" drawn out in her Utah vernacular that made it real to me. Pregnant at twenty-three with her fifth kid, she set him free because she had double-crossed him, black eyes and beatings aside.

The day Mother and Stepdad brought Sal home from the hospital, we were still in Utah and the snow was deep and high and covered the remaindered wood that was piled up by the front door. Wood that we got from the lumberyard across the alley and used for heating the house and for cooking on the cast-iron stove in the kitchen.

Sal was wrapped in a blue woven blanket with matching satin ribbon all around it. He was a blue-ribbon bundle in Stepdad's arms. Snow piled on the collar of Stepdad's Union Pacific Railroad winter coat when he walked up the walkway with Sal. Mother walked beside him, her hospital bag in hand along with Sal's baby bag. Stepdad tracked in boot-cut sooty snow when he walked through the door.

"Remember, Tony," Mother said. "You come back, you accept my child."

Both of them walked inside the door to the shack where we lived next to the lumberyard, and Stepdad held Sal up in the middle of the room and offered him to our family. "This is your new brother," he said. "He is the new baby now."

He walked Sal over to the crib and laid him down behind the wooden slats. Sal's little fists pushed against the walls of his blanket. But soon enough he settled, at once at rest, as though it was just enough to be there.

"Like I told you, you come back, you accept my child," Mother repeated.

He did. Stepdad kept his word. He never told Sal he wasn't his. Sal got as many beatings as—certainly not measurably more than—we all got, Stepdad's kid or not, except Ted, who never got hit. No hint. Not a clue. With his split-tooth smile, Stepdad kept his word.

By the time Sal came home from the hospital, there were already four of us. He was the second of the three December babies, born a year apart three Decembers in a row.

That December when Mother and Stepdad brought Sal home from the hospital, Mother had cleaned all the windows in the house. The cast-iron potbelly stove in the kitchen both cooked our food and kept us warm. Mother lifted the heavy metal round burners to throw in odd-shaped pieces of wood from the lumberyard scrap heap she'd send us out for. She hooked a metal pole into a groove in the round cast-iron plate that fit cookie-cutter into its shape in the stove. The oven door opened the whole width of the right side. Inside, flames curled heat through the holes at the bottom of the oven. She always kept a pot of beans going. The smell laid around the house in sweet steam that dripped down the windows.

"We'll never be hungry as long as we've got a sack of beans and a sack of rice in this house," Mother said.

Brown poop was smeared on the slats of Sal's crib, in Sal's hair, on his face, and all over the crib sheets. Sal was starting to fling poop on the floor outside the crib.

Mother sat by the window she'd wiped clean. She stared out at the snow and flinched at the flakes as they landed on the ledge.

She closed her eyes, rocking herself back and forth against the window. More snow landed, and when she opened her eyes, the mounting flakes made her rock faster.

Mother sat on a cornflower bedsheet next to the window with buttered Wonder bread in her hand, the window being closed in on by the advancing snowflakes. She stuffed a bit of bread in her mouth. Piece by piece, she ate the bread, and she continued to rock as the snowflakes closed in on her. My brothers and I pulled ourselves into each other to fit in the doorway to watch her.

"What are you kids looking at?" she asked, her mouth full.

We got so small together that we became a ball. Mother rocked back and forth on the couch under the window, rolling and stuffing more bread into her mouth.

From under the bedsheet, she pulled out a hanger. The wire was bent and stretched out of its triangle into a crooked square, and the head was curved into a beak. Mother and her bird beak hook were on us.

"Goddammit, I'll give you something to stare at," she said.

We got tighter and tighter into our ball and rolled around and around in the path we cut through the doorways between the three rooms. She'd gain on us, and we'd lap her. She laughed and swung at us. We'd lap her again. Finally, she shut one of the doors. We got tighter into our ball and bounced off the door. She hid behind the door and gouged the air with her beak-hooked hanger and laughed. She laughed and laughed.

Her laugh changed like it all had been a game. We got close to her and started to unravel, close enough to touch her. She pulled her hanger out and came after us. We bunched up and ran. Sal stood up in his crib, poop in his hair, and started to cry.

Mother stopped. The snowflakes had piled up on the window so that the very last bit of light was gone. She dropped her hanger and pulled the cornflower sheet up to the window to rub the snow off from the inside of the window, but the snow wouldn't go away. The harder she rubbed, the higher it got.

The inside of Sal's leg was covered with a new line of poop. He pushed it through the crib slats. Poop was now on the floor. She leaned over the crib slats and put her hands under his arms to lift him without getting any on her.

"As for you," Mother said, lifting Sal up as his feet kicked poop everywhere. "As for you."

She wrapped a blanket around him and took him into the kitchen and laid him on the cutting board. She opened his blanket and positioned Sal in the middle of it. She pulled one blue-ribbon blanket corner over him, and then another, and another, until she had folded Sal up like a package. She rolled him back and forth like she was kneading dough until he was folded up tight.

"As for you," she repeated.

She pulled down the porcelain handle on the oven door. The hinge creaked open. The oven heat broke into the cold air around us. She pulled out the oven grate. She took the blue bundle from the cutting board to the open oven door and laid Sal on the grate. Sal's foot broke out of his packaged fold and hit the blue porcelain oven wall. He shrieked. He shrieked so loud that Mother pulled him off the grate and dropped him on the floor next to the hanger. Sal broke all the way out of his bundle and lay there, crying and screaming so loud that Mother snapped awake and ran back to the window and curled up under the cornflower bedsheet until the snowflakes pelted her to sleep.

When Great-Grandma Mercedes found us, we had dragged Sal away from the stove and closed the oven door.

"Margarita," Mercedes said as she walked over to Mother. "*Despiertate.*" *Wake up.*

Mercedes picked Sal up, put him in the sink, and washed him clean, rubbing lard on his burnt foot and changing him into a fresh diaper. She tore bits of tortilla to put into our *frijoles de la olla* bean soup and sat us at the table to eat. Tortilla bits floated in the soup with our plump beans. Sal was back in his wiped-clean crib on fresh sheets.

Mercedes walked over to Mother who sat under the corn-flowers by the window, and, flower by flower, Mercedes pulled the cornflowers off Mother, using words only I could under-stand, because she spoke them in Spanish, my first language, which I learned from Mercedes.

"Listen to me," she said to Mother. "These are your kids, goddamn it. You better go where you have to go and find what you have to find to get yourself ready to take care of them. They are yours and no one else's. You wanted them, and then you took the girl from me. There was no immaculate conception to birth them, and there isn't going to be any miracle to raise them."

Mother rocked and nodded with buttered Wonder bread rolled up in her hand.

When my son was a baby and Mother came to visit me, I put her in the same room with him in my college married-student housing apartment. My son, like my brother, would later reveal the pattern of bipolar behaviors that I now identify in Mother's violent mood swings and depressions. My baby son was crying, and I got up to see Mother standing over him with the same malice and fear I saw in her when I was a child. I grabbed my son, out of fear of the harm I'd seen her inflict, and moved him away from her.

CHAPTER 7

CANNED FISH

With Tres Flores Brilliantine hair tonic in his hair and railroad tar thick in his pant thighs, he tracked in boot-cut mud all the way up our red steps, across the black-and-white foyer, over Mother's polished hardwood, and into the yellow linoleum kitchen. I had to call him Dad, but he wasn't my dad, he was my brothers' dad.

With a split-tooth smile, he handed us our forks for our dinner. We ate out of a can of weird-looking fish named Dolores.

Cold fish jelly slipped around on our tongues, making it difficult to eat the chunks of light and dark meat stabbed cold out of the can, but we had to, bone and all. Some days we couldn't eat it and it was our fault. Our fault because we couldn't see the beautiful Mexican coastline of Sinaloa, because we couldn't smell the ocean, and because all we had was the bug-infested Great Salt Lake.

On Easter morning, camera in hand, Stepdad cut our silhouette into a family portrait against the abandoned house next door where Bloody Bones lived. In Utah we called her Bloody Bones; in Mexico she is La Llorona.

The mythic Mexican crying woman, La Llorona drowned her children when her husband left her for another woman. In her rage, she held her children's heads, one by one, under clear stream water until their bodies floated like buoys. In her grief at having drowned them, she is doomed to roam in search of them for eternity and can be heard calling out for them.

"*Hijos*," she cries.

Mexicans throughout the diaspora hear her cry for all lost children. Her ghost searches for them like Mexico itself in search of the children it killed, lost, or sent away.

In our family portrait, my Easter dress is a blue embossed crinoline with short sleeves, a full skirt, and a bow in the back. Shipped by rail up from Mexico City, the skirt was long enough to cover my unsightly knees, scrubbed raw from the horse brush they used to wash us with, and my hair was twisted into ringlets under a matching Easter bonnet.

"Say cheese," Stepdad instructed.

Joe and Ted were a full half-foot shorter than I was and stood close to me in white tweed Sunday suits. We closed our teeth and spread our lips to cover the sound of cheese.

Click.

The other three kids stood in front of us in little boy short pants suits, their little hands closed into baby fists. With our backs to Bloody's, we knew she waited in search of children to steal, cut up, and eat.

Another *click*.

Haunted or condemned, one wrong step inside Bloody's could send you deep, deep into a hole to nowhere. With his camera in hand, Stepdad's back was to the Coca-Cola bottling company across the street with its big sparkling red-and-white Coca-Cola sign that went on and off all day and night.

"Estan estill," Stepdad said.

Stepdad held his black square box camera in two hands to balance us in his viewer against the light and dark of Bloody's house. His head down, his voice up.

"Say cheese," he said.

"Cheese!" we said.

Click.

In back of Bloody's, an old Hudson sat on cinder blocks, all dressed up and bow-tie ready in shiny chrome and industrial green. The suicide doors opened to silver woven tapestry fish that swam up and down the diamond tuck seats. Surrounded by metal, we sat in his lap, Easter baskets in hand, our faces against the fabric. The Hudson was our old man, the neighborhood grandpa.

When it wasn't Easter, we dared the Mormons from down the block to meet us in front of Bloody's. With their pink noses in the Snickers box we offered them, they got a good whiff of a turd disguised as a Snickers bar that we had fished fresh out of our toilet to nowhere on the backyard loading dock that morning. They dropped the turd on Bloody's rotted wood porch.

"Dirty Mexicans." They started up into Bloody's after us but stopped, too afraid to come inside. "Goddamn dirty Mexicans!" the Mormons yelled, running off.

We hung, elbows out, from Bloody's upstairs window, next to the leftover rolls of wallpaper, paint, and wood planks that our parents had planned to put into Bloody's before having to leave it behind.

We headed to the Hudson to sit with the tapestry fish and brought along a hardened railroad salvage, a Snickers bar from our backyard warehouse where Stepdad stored all the stuff he brought home from the railroad track. The Snickers was so old that the chocolate had started to ash and we needed a chisel to cut it five ways.

On regular days, when our mother sent us out of our world and into theirs, our shirts and blouses were pressed and starched stiff against our backs, our knees and elbows were horse-hair-brushed clean, and our toasted Wonder bread was buttered and ready to eat.

Mother brought our clothes home piled high in stacks of blue wrappers tied up with string from the laundry where she worked.

The owners ignored the "LDS only" rule for the shift that came and went in the night. When she wasn't pushing laundry sheets through big rolling irons, with our shirts laid in between, Mother lived in a yellow seersucker housedress. It was pinned top to bottom with three chipped-nose, blue-eyed, yellow ducky diaper pins. When she talked, all you could see was the cavity between her two front teeth.

"Get in here!" she called at us, broom in hand, from the top of the red steps to the bungalow. Home for lunch, we met her at the bottom of the steps with our hands over our heads to duck Stepdad's dried boot-cut mud that she sent out just over our heads from her broom.

"What the hell took you kids so long?" she said.

It was a slow climb up the red steps to her school day lunch diluted from a can of Campbell's tomato soup. The kids on the empty can of Campbell's soup couldn't help their slaphappy, "Mmm, mmm, good" faces from smiling at us from the garbage can.

"Don't slam that door!" Mother called at us from inside where she dished out our bowls of soup. Door slamming set her on edge, and when she got really rattled, she ate long green slithery asparagus out of the can, can after can.

We sat down around the yellow Formica table with the fat-cheeked and happy Campbell's soup kids staring at us from the can label, their faces plastered with that dopey, happy look that made you just want to beat the shit out of 'em.

Mother's lips opened and closed over the sliver of rot between her teeth.

"Siddown 'n' eat," she said.

His eyes as big as saucers with cherries settled at the bottom, Jose Roberto pushed up to the yellow Formica. We called him Jozay or Hosey, but mostly he was just Joe. The collar on his blue starched shirt was creased with lines up the side of it. Pressed flat through Mother's rolling iron, our shirts were creased in places where nobody else had creases. Under the rippled chrome that surrounded the yellow Formica kitchen table, Joe started to pick at his shirt buttons like he was picking at a scab.

"Eat yer goddamn soup," Mother said.

Joe's spoon dove for the onion he hated and knew was hidden in his soup. He scab-picked each button up his shirt and started picking at his collar button.

"I said to eat yer soup," Mother said again.

Joe stirred until the saltines were red and swollen and had lost their salty shine.

In her seersucker and yellow duckies, Mother leaned into Joe.

"I said to eat," she repeated.

Joe wrapped his arm around his bowl and hunched over it, stirring faster.

"Find it?" Mother asked. "Find yer goddamn onion?"

Her hand on the back of his head, Joe circled tighter around his bowl, just a nose away from his soup.

"Goddamn it, eat!" she told him. "Goddamn you, eat it."

Duckies pressed against his starched, crooked shirt collar, she pushed Joe's face into the red soup. "From now on, when I tell you to eat, I mean for you to eat yer goddamn food," she said.

Tomato soup dripped from Joe's eyelids and spread into red circles on the blue starched cotton. Joe choked out his soup. Mother and the duckies closed in.

"Goddamn worthless piece of shit, when I tell you to eat, you eat, you hear me?" she said.

Joe brought the soup up to his lips, but his lips wobbled so bad, he couldn't open his mouth.

"Damn it to hell, get the hell away from this table and get upstairs and put on a clean shirt," she told him.

"The rest of you, hurry up and eat, and get the hell out of here before you're late for school."

We waited for Joe out back in the warehouse, at the loading dock just outside our kitchen pantry. We stood by the railroad salvage from the track, broken-up boxes of candy, soap, bent soup and vegetable cans, folded copper wire, railroad ties, cast-off toilets, and whatever else fell off the train. The Mormons who'd lived in our house before us had jury-rigged a warehouse over our backyard for food hoarding and distribution. Our play in the warehouse backyard was in the dark, lit only by cracks in the makeshift roof. It was where dirt, rocks, broken glass, and stray bricks governed our steps. Outside the wooden warehouse doors was our alley, where we'd go the back way to school.

As we waited for Joe by the empty, bent-in-half Jolly Green Giant Niblets corn cans, we took turns stomping the dopey, happy Campbell's soup kids. We liked the giant, so we didn't stomp him. Joe's eyes moved back and forth at the bottom of his eye socket as we walked with him through the alley. We kicked him a can that we'd saved for him for the way back up South West Temple to school, but he just kept walking, hiding his face in his freshly ironed, crooked collar. At the end of the alley, we propped the can up on a rock against the fence and took turns kicking its stomach in.

When I wasn't in school, I got out of the house when I could through the alley to go to the store past the big trashy yard on the corner where the family of Mormon kids lived. They were "Jack-Mormons," slang for lapsed, nominally claimed by the Mormons but in need of saving. We were Jack-Mexicans: claimed by no one, and beyond saving. We paid the price for salvation but could never get to heaven.

When I got back, Stepdad was in the kitchen with an open yellow can of food. He had the belt out.

"Where you been?" he asked.

"You said I could go." My voice sounded small in the large kitchen doorway.

"You supposed to stay in the yard," he said.

He grabbed my hair, gripping it tightly in one of his hands. My hair was strong enough for him to use it as a rope to drag me around the kitchen, and the skin on my back and arms was thick enough to rise into long red lines from belt whips from his other hand. From under the yellow Formica table, with my arms wrapped around its long, curved chrome leg, my one good eye rolled over to a can with a blue, green, and pink wide-finned fish flying out of the sea into the blue, blue sky.

"From now on, you stay in the yard." The belt buckle hung loose as he pulled the rest of the belt around him.

I found our dog, Pizzie, under the red steps in the cool dirt. His short white hair was covered with odd-shaped black spots that looked like misshapen moles, some flat and some bumpy. His left eye was brown and his right eye black.

"Come here, boy," I said. "C'mere."

He came to me.

When he got close, just past the broken lattice, I sent him back to his circle of rags.

"Come here, boy," I called him back. "Here, Piz."

He came to me. His wet nose shined. I pushed him away.

"Come here, boy," I called him back again. "Come on, boy."

His flanks pushed back and forth. He stopped close enough to sniff my raised red skin and the skinny scabs on my knees from the horsehair brushing, but he didn't look up. Even when he stopped looking up, I knew he'd come back every time I sent him away.

The screen door slammed flat against its dirty white frame. Mother's voice cracked with the door.

"I told you to get in here," Mother said.

My legs moved, muscle against bone.

"Get down to the goddamn store and get me a can of tomato sauce. I gotta make some rice. Who knows what the hell you kids have been eating," she said.

I walked by the house of Mormon kids who lived at the end of our block across the street from the store, and waited at the light.

The corner-store grocer's eyes moved up and down the raised red skin on my arms and my closed eye when I reached across the counter to give him the money. He pressed the copper penny change into my hand, and with his hand he folded my fingers around the coins, holding my closed fist in his two hands. I pulled away, copper against tin, threw the change into the sack, and choked it tightly enough to open a brown paper flower on top of the red Hunt's tomato sauce can.

Paper flower in hand, I prayed at the altar of school supplies, like I did every time I went to the store. This time the grocer was too busy to walk me to the door. New yellow Ticonderoga pencils, pink erasers, scissors, protractors, and lined paper took up the whole wall by the door.

I opened my paper sack flower and stuffed in another handful of yellow pencils before walking slowly out the door. The shiny green metal eraser bands stuck out of my fist all the way home. Just outside our front gate, I threw the pencils into the big bush in Bloody Bones's yard with the other ones.

Upstairs in my room on my bench by the window was where I kept an eye on my pencils and watched out for Bloody Bones. It was also where I opened my ink-blue Baltimore Catechism to newsprint questions about God. I read them out loud.

"Who made me?"

"God made me."

"Jesus was his only begotten son."

"Holy Catholic and Apostolic," I read.

MOTHER WAS HAPPY WHEN SHE BAKED. She tied on a red rick-rack apron over her yellow seersucker. In her three-pocket apron skirt, there were bottles of red, green, yellow, and blue sprinkles in the first pocket; cookie cutters shaped into moons, cats, Easter eggs, Uncle Sam hats, and firecrackers in the middle pocket. In the last pocket were several child-size red-handled wooden rolling pins poking out against the red rickrack.

"*A-tisket, a-tasket, I lost my yellow basket,*" Mother sang to us as she rolled out cookie dough. "*Was it blue?*"

We joined her in our part of the song. "*No, no, no, no, no, no.*"

"*Was it green? Was it purple? Was it pink? Was it violet? Was it chartreuse?*"

We sang "*no, no, no*" to each color, until Mother finished the song with, "*I found it, I found it. I found my yellow basket.*"

All the dough was rolled out, Easter egg and bunny cookies, cut round and ready. Mother's back was to me, and the big bow tied on the back of her apron pushed against the yellow Formica when she bent over to open the oven door.

"Mom?" I asked.

"Yes?" she said, handing me a cookie sheet.

"Mom, what is 'beloved'?"

"What? Pay attention here," she said.

"Mom, the catechism says that Jesus is 'beloved,'" I explained.

"Yeah. And?" she replied.

"That word sounds kind of funny to me, like it's not even a word," I said.

Cookie sheets on the table, Mother pulled back the butter wrapper to the first red line on the cube. "Here, grease this pan," she instructed.

She pushed my buttery fingers into the corners of the cookie sheet. "And get those edges right."

"It kind of made me laugh when I read it," I said.

My hand under the dough, the cookies got laid out on the sheet.

"Mom, see?" I put my buttered finger on the catechism newsprint word *beloved*. "How can somebody be 'be loved'?"

Mother slid the sheets into the oven, undid her apron, and folded it over the oven door handle. "It just means God loves Jesus, for Chrissake, that's all. Now go upstairs and wash your hands," she said.

Mother walked the flour bag out to the pantry that led to the loading dock out back to the warehouse.

"Who shit in this goddam toilet?" Mother called from the warehouse.

I took my butter-smeared catechism book to the red steps out front where, next door, Mr. Binder was painting a bike. His pink paintbrush followed the curves on one of two bike fenders. The whitewall tires were lined up underneath his workbench, and the side grill said *Schwinn.*

"What are you doin', Mr. Binder?" I asked.

"Oh, I'm paintin' a bike," he replied.

"It sure is a pretty bike," I said.

"It sure is."

"Who's it for?"

"I can't rightly say, darlin'."

Mr. Binder pointed his brush toward the kitchen and moved his hat to block the sun.

"Just never you mind and get back to yer studyin'," he said.

In the living room, Stepdad was singing as Marty Robbins played from the record player radio with big speakers on each side and a shelf for records.

"*A white sport coat and a pink carnation.*"

For his First Holy Communion, Stepdad bought Joe an all-white suit and a bow tie. Dad put a white carnation in Joe's lapel and worked some Brylcreem, "a little dab'll do ya," into Joe's hair. The radio was on, and Stepdad sang while he combed Joe's hair with a skinny black comb.

"*A white sport coat and a pink carnation . . .*" Stepdad curved Joe's hair up just so, Joe's cheeks pink and his eyes wide open. In the middle of his First Communion picture, Joe sat on Father Connolly's lap. The rest of the First Communion boys in their black suits made a frame around Father and Joe.

Joe started to wake up in the morning with big wet circles on his sheets; there was a yellow edge where the sheet had started to dry. He put his cowboy pajamas on the heater and waited, crying. Now everything smelled like burnt pee. He knew he was going to get it because now Mother had to run the sheets through the ringer washer and flat iron them in the big rolling irons all over again.

Mother's yellow duckies were tangled in the black coil telephone line downstairs.

"Get upstairs and get me your brother's blue shirt," Mother said.

The coil cut a diagonal line between her breasts and stomach while she talked to Aunt Dora on the phone.

"I told you to get up there," she told me.

Her back to me, I stood next to her with the blue shirt.

"Jesus Christ, I'm pregnant again," she said into the black receiver.

She turned to see me and motioned me away.

"I'm going to need you here to watch these kids when I go to the hospital," she said into the phone.

I went upstairs and brought down another shirt and stood next to her.

"Not that goddamn shirt, you idiot," she said. "Don't make me have to go up there, because if I find that shirt, I am going to beat the shit out of you, you hear me?"

I brought back the blue one.

"I don't know what the hell took you so long," she complained. "Now get a move on, you kids are going to be late for school."

ON THE WAY TO SCHOOL, TED started crying because his hands were cold. We called him Tomas Eduardo or Tommy Ed or just Ted. In our family portrait, Stepdad dressed him in an olive cable-knit pullover to show off his deep-brown skin and his black, black hair. Now, covered in snow, his hair fell into a peak in the middle of his forehead.

"Here," I said. I took his hand, put it in my pocket, and pushed his other hand into his coat sleeve. "Grab the inside of your sleeve," I told him.

He grabbed it and stuck it in his pocket.

"Did you see the bike Mr. Binder is painting?" I asked him. His eyes, welled red, got clear. "It's a girl's bike," he said. "I know."

"Who do you think it's for?" he asked, his nose running.

"I don't know," I said, "but my birthday is coming up."

"Do you think it's for you?" he said, snow settling in the snot on his face.

"I don't think so. It might be, but don't say anything," I said.

After school, Ted pushed open the gate by the pencil bush and ran up the red steps. "Mom, Mom, Sis is going to get a bike!" he told Mother.

"How the hell? How do you know?" Mother asked him.

"Sis told me," he replied, his black bird beak pecking back at me.

The yellow duckies on Mother's dress pushed against the screen door before it flew open.

"Did your aunt open her mouth about that bike?" Mother demanded.

The screen door slammed flat against the house.

"No," I said, making my way up the red steps.

"Well, who the hell told?" Mother wanted to know.

"Nobody," I said.

The duckies were pulled end to end in the yellow seersucker stretched to cover Mother's growing stomach when our aunt showed up on the day of the parade. She wore a white shift with fringe that moved back and forth across her bust and hips when she stepped into our black-and-white foyer. Her hair was shellacked into a flip, and she was holding the glittery plastic handle of a pink portable record player. Her white slingback pumps tapped across the hardwood floor. She flipped up the silver latch and snapped pink plastic disc holders into a stack of 45s. Her lips, painted in pink lipstick, opened and closed over the words, and she pulled us around her.

"*Can I walk you ho-ome?*" she sang to us.

Her white pumps leading us, we moved, foot back, foot forward, and elbow inside elbow, in a centipede to the Stroll. Our feet moved on the black-and-white tiles in a perfect square for the Foursquare, and our backs straight, shoulder to shoulder, we leaned into the Walk. The last 45 automatically dropped from the stack into the Peppermint Twist.

"Move your foot," she instructed, "like you're putting out a cigarette."

Smoking was a sin, but we did it anyway, stopping only slightly to lift and point, our toes pivoting on one spot, and then another, so that we could Twist and Twist and Twist.

Just outside our front gate, people lined chairs up and down the block with their backs to Bloody's, our house, and the Coca-Cola bottling company across the street, all the way up to the corner house and the corner store. Stepdad walked up and down the length of our front gate with his camera in hand as he balanced everybody in his moving viewer.

Click.

Click.

The grand marshal of the Mormon Pioneer Day Parade was the Rifleman himself, Chuck Connors, and his TV son Mark. They sat in a Cadillac convertible that moved slowly in front of the blinking Coca-Cola sign. Next to Connors on the white leather seat was quiet, steady, obedient Mark, every parent's good boy. His black hat in hand, Mark waved at us as he went by our gate. I was certain that he saw me from where I stood next to my pencil bush. My crease-crooked blouse was wet under my arms and on my back.

When the parade was over, our aunt closed the pink box, flipped up the silver latch, and walked us down the red steps, past the pencil bush, out of the gate, and down two blocks to the Twist contest at the Safeway parking lot.

Her white-fringed shift swung back and forth when she twisted her hips. She did the Peppermint Twist, the Spanish

Twist, the Florida Twist, and every other kind of Twist you could do. With a curve of sweat under her arms, she Twisted everybody off the parking lot.

When the contest was over, she stood next to the podium in front of piles and piles of peaches, plums, cherries, and apricots to hear the prize announcement. The ward bishop who managed the Safeway stood in front of the podium to hand out the prizes, a dirty line of sweat running down the side of his crew-cut head and spilling into a growing spot on his white shirt collar. Kid after kid lined up in front of our aunt, prizes in hand, as the ward bishop called for another box of prizes. The further back she got, the more her Aqua Net flip started to drip against the apricots, cherries, plums, and peaches. Pretty soon you couldn't see her at all, and the prize box was empty.

My friends were outside and Stepdad was asleep. Dolores the fish, in her yellow can, sat on his bedside table. The starched-stiff sheets had been broken up by his sleep and fell into layers on Step-dad like the white sheets fell on my uncle Ray when he was asleep. Stepdad turned in his sleep, his Tres Flores hair falling over his forehead against the pillow. There were lines on his cheek from the pink chenille he was sleeping on. I lifted the sheet and the chenille, the way my uncle Ray liked me to when he was sleeping. My uncle Ray lived at my great-grandma Mercedes's house, where I lived before my mother came in a police car to take me away. I wanted to be nice like my uncle Ray said to be nice so I could go out and play. The way I used to be nice for my uncle Ray.

Stepdad pulled himself and his sheet out of his sleep.

"What de hell you doing?" he asked, walking kind of spindly-legged to the door. "Get the hell out of here!" he said.

He walked fast. His bare feet against the wooden floor, he gathered his sheet around him like a cloud.

My pink bike was missing.

"We saw it," Ted said. He pointed his beak-shaped head to the corner. "The Mormon kids on the corner have it."

My bike wasn't pink anymore. It had black primer on the fenders, but the Schwinn writing was the same.

Just past the gate, the Schwinn's black fender rode past the pencil bush. The oldest Mormon boy was on the bike. The Schwinn turned into the house on the corner across the street from the store.

When Stepdad got home from work, he parked his lunch bucket and work boots on the top red step. Joe pushed his short legs up to where Dad sat. He looked up at Stepdad but couldn't talk. A serrated can lid folded back over a picture of white, pulpy food. It was a fish that didn't look like fish, called abalone. Stepdad speared it and bit the chunk on his fork.

"Wha' so matta?" Stepdad said.

"Wha' happen to the bike?" Stepdad asked.

Joe rolled his eyes in the direction of the corner where the Mormon kids lived.

"Come on," Stepdad said, pulling Joe by the hand. "Let's go."

The rule was simple: nobody ripped you off without a fight. Even if you knew you were going to lose, you had to make it cost them too. So even if you ended up in the dirt, trashed or beat up, you had to do your own damage, because then maybe the next time they would think twice before they came after you, and besides, anything could happen.

Joe headed up the sidewalk to the corner house where the Mormon kids lived. I stood outside the gate and grabbed my pencils from the pencil bush, ready to go too.

"You stay in the yard," Stepdad told me.

Whatever piece of himself my brother found to take with him that day, he found it, on his way, on that slow walk up the block, to the end of that street.

When he got home, his eye was swollen shut and his nose was full of blood. His clothes were torn. He ran up the red stairs and threw open the screen door. The door slammed square against its dirty white frame behind him, and he walked right past Mother.

Two days later, my bike showed up in the back under the warehouse wall. The fenders were gone, and there was a boy's seat, not a girl's seat, on it, but it still said *Schwinn*. We rolled the bike up the red steps to the porch and waited for Stepdad to come home. Stepdad handed us his lunch bucket. There were no railroad salvage Mars bars, or Milky Ways, or the stuff he sometimes found for us on the track. There was only a half-open can of one of his fishes. Behind the screen door in the house, Mother was talking on the phone so fast that if you were close to her, you wouldn't be able to see the rot between her teeth. The new baby was crying.

"The windows on the Hudson have been broken out," she said. "There is glass everywhere. The seats have been ripped out. They saw some Mexican kids out there."

Stepdad loosened his work boots, picked his can out of his lunch bucket, rolled back the lid, and stuck his fork in it.

We pulled off his boots and sat next to Stepdad with Pizzie at our feet. Stepdad stared out over the yard like he could see all the way to the ocean.

"You guys tear up the Hudson?" Stepdad asked.

My brothers looked sideways at each other.

Stepdad took another bite of his fish.

"You guys kill the old man?" he asked.

Joe turned his head and looked ready to roll his eyes up to Stepdad.

"Es okay," Stepdad said.

He took the last bite out of his can.

"Es okay. We getting de hell out o dis place."

CHAPTER 8

THAT'S HOW YOU CLEAN A FLOOR

My hair hung over and mixed in with the soot on my face, briny sweat trimming my mouth. My job was to clean the back porch of the one-bedroom fourplex we had just moved into, our first home in South Central LA. The mop stick held me up as I hunched over it. The rag mop made of cut-up old school blouses and towels slid across the washed-out yellow-and-white linoleum. The faded green back door swung shut, its latch jangling. Flies moved in and out of the torn screen, sometimes landing on my face.

"Did you fill that bucket with hot water?" my mother called from the kitchen.

"Yes, Mom," I replied, my voice moving slower than the mop.

"Make sure that water is hot," she said.

I dabbed my fingers into the pail.

"Don't make me have to come over there to check that water," she said. "You'll be sorry if I have to go check that water."

"It's hot, Mom." I dragged the mop deeper into the floor.

"Well, get busy and start moppin' that floor. Make sure you get all the corners. This place is filthy. We're going to get it clean if it takes all day."

The clothes I'd just hung in the backyard snapped and swayed in the wind on lines that hung heavy in the middle anchored by leaning poles. Wet towels missed the dirt by inches and started to dry under the hot sun. The backyard was hard, with glints of glass, metal and rock, like bumpy metal flake Formica. Lemon-scented Tide wafted over the hot lines into the back porch. Broken glass, tin cans, rocks, and dirt reflected small bits of light. I could hear the kids, my five brothers coming home from the corner store through the alley.

"Mom said you can't have any because you peed last night," Ted said, clutching a bag that held lemon-lime Kool-Aid, seven slices of bologna, Wonder bread, and a twenty-nine-cent bag of Clover Club potato chips.

"No, she didn't," Joe said.

"Yes, she did."

"Didn't."

"Did too, ask her."

They moved up the back stairs to the porch.

"Don't come in," I said, and blocked the doorway with the mop. "Go around. I'm mopping."

"I can't," Joe replied, clutching his crotch. "I have to pee now."

"Too bad," I said, fixing the swing lock on the door. "Go around."

"Mommm!" he called, now jumping up and down.

"What's the matter?" The hallway door to the kitchen hit the wall. Mother came in.

"She won't let me in." He pointed to me, both hands on his crotch, his voice moving up and down with him in higher and higher decibels.

Mother slapped up the swing lock and waved the boys over the half-mopped floor.

"You haven't even gotten started yet," she told me. "Hurry up. Let me see that mop." She broke my hold on the mop when she yanked it from me. "You haven't even swept in here yet."

"I did, Mom," I insisted.

"What's that under the water heater?" she said. The shrill timbre of her voice stabbed me in the gut, in that place where she knew she could hit hard enough to hurt. She pointed to the encrusted dirt in the corner wall under the water heater.

"I couldn't reach that, Mom," I said.

"Get down there and scrape that out."

"I tried. The dirt's too hard, Mom."

Mother threw a half bucket of hot water under the water heater.

"Hook up this hose under the sink," she called to Joe, throwing him a black rubber tube, "and hold it under the faucet until I tell you to let go."

"Now, you," she said, pointing to me, "get down there with the mop stick and scrape that out."

I crouched down, holding the mop stick between my legs, and hit the mountain of dirt with the blunt end of the mop stick. Slightly softened, the dirt started to cake while Mother pressed the steady stream of water against it. Chunks of dirt started to break loose. The cat that sat on the fence jumped off and ran under the porch.

Layer after layer washed through my legs. All the dirt. The dirt on my face. My black hair. My mother's dirt. Dirt I didn't even know about yet. Dirt and more dirt. Dirt that made you dirty. Dirt that made you Mexican. Dirt that made you poor. Dirt that made you feel like so much dirt. Dirt that turned into dirt's dirt. Not dirty dirt, but just dirt, dirt that made you want to eat dirt, haul dirt, gather dirt, hoard dirt. Dirt to plant plants in. Dirt to hold houses up. Dirt that made you whole.

A noise escaped from behind the water heater.

"A rat!" I screamed, jumping back and then lunging forward with the mop stick.

"Get 'im!" Ted called from the doorway.

A large rat brushed my ankle and ran across the room to the door. Trapped in the door, the rat tried to scale it, but the latch held firm. Finally, it made through the rip in the screen.

"What happened?" Joe called from the kitchen. His hands choked the black hose over the faucet.

"Sis caught a rat!" Ted's eyes ricocheted as he clung to the doorway to the hall.

I continued to scrape out the dirt with the stick, hitting lumps of dirt until I could only hit the floor and wall under and behind the water heater. I hit and hit until I couldn't stop. Another rat limped out and tumbled along in the hot stream. This one had a small pink rat in its mouth. Finally, several more small pink baby rats fell out end over end with the water. In all, they counted seven pink baby rats—or pieces of rat—flow through the back porch.

Mother stopped the hose, and some of the boys ran after the rat with a broomstick. The cat came in, and Joe and Ted followed him to see where he was taking the baby rats. Down on our hands and knees, Mother and I continued to scrape and clean the floor under the water heater until it was a brighter shade of white and yellow than the rest of the floor.

Mother hand-wrung the mop and hung the bucket. "That's how you clean a floor," she said. "Now bring the towels in."

CHAPTER 9

DR. ROSS' DOG FOOD

In Sister Agatha's fourth-grade class at St. Turibius Catholic School in South Central LA, somebody drew a mustache on the Holy Mother. The black line was wide and bushy and covered most of her porcelain pink lip. It wasn't thin and narrow like the mustache on El Catrín in our Lotería game. Not thin like the pinstripes on his pants. The Holy Mother's mustache was wide and flat like somebody had taken a marker, wanting to give her a mustache and *mocos*, snots too.

In her corner by the door, the Holy Mother's blue veiled arms opened to ceramic lambs that flocked around her. When she started to wear a mustache, new things appeared in the altar under her robed feet: marbles, jacks, barrettes, rabbits' feet, vinyl key chains, and a chicharron.

Sister Agatha tried to rub the mustache off, but it wouldn't come off, so she put a veil over the Holy Mother's head. The Holy Mother sat in her corner with her arms open, her head tilted slightly, her mustache visible through her lace, surrounded by all of her offerings.

The red plaid pleats of my uniform opened like an accordion over my knees. We sat in curved wooden chairs that were bolted to the floor. The sides of our desks were made of wrought iron, the black iron shaped into a filigree design that joined our desk to the chair. The top of our desk was hardwood, and it was hinged to the rest of the desk and opened for storage of our books, paper, and pencils. There was a carved-in space for pencils, and a hole for an inkwell.

Jesus hung there like he always did, on the cross in front of us on the wall, in his pastel-orange shrine. He was always bleeding and sad, with thorns sticking up around his head. His head was lowered under the INRI sign that the Romans hung above him on the cross.

Sister Agatha walked in.

Twenty-five skirts folded into standing knife-edged pleats, and twenty-five pairs of cords stood like stalks over boys' legs.

"Good morning, Sister Agatha," we said.

Sister Agatha took a step up to the platform where her desk was, her hands in front of her like she was getting ready to open a book for our lesson. Her black-and-brown wool skirt muffled the sounds of her key and rosary tapping when she lifted her other black shoe to the wooden platform.

Sister Agatha walked to the middle of the platform. Her eyes were red, and her pink face was puffy like it was trying to escape the white starched box she wore over her forehead and down the sides of her face. Her black veil covered the top of her head and hung in folds around the parts of her face not covered by the box. Her red skin pushed against the stiff linen, and Sister's blue eyes looked like they had been shot out of a marble game by one of my brother's steelies. There was no book in her hand, and she put her hands together like she was going to pray.

"Children, please be seated and give me your full attention," Sister said.

I lifted the top of my desk and took out my lunch sack, rolling it in my hands. The paper sack was rolled so tight that the sandwich was as long as the rolled-up handle. The potato chips were smashed in the baggie next to the wax paper–covered bologna sandwich. Mayonnaise, one piece of lettuce, and a slice of bologna had marinated the whole morning for that just-right taste.

Sister pulled her rosary out of the side of her habit and held it in front of her in her left hand. She touched the crucifix that hung around her neck with her right hand.

"Children," she said, "our president, John Fitzgerald Kennedy, is dead."

Sister's eyelids fell like curtains over her blue marble eyes.

"Let us pray," she said.

I unrolled my hand from around my lunch sack to free up my choked sandwich and spread my palms together palm to palm as hard as I could to pray. We all dropped to our knees.

"Hail Mary, full of grace, the Lord is with thee . . ."

Sister finished out the rest of whatever she added on to our prayers and put her rosary back in her black-and-brown skirt. I got up from the floor and brushed the dust off my red knees.

"Class is dismissed," she said. "You are to go straight home to your families."

I grabbed my lunch and went to wait for my brothers in front of the Sacred Heart of Jesus statue. Jesus's hand opened to the red heart on his chest that pumped red and yellow. I waited for my brothers so we could go home together like we always did. They came in from all directions and bunched up around Jesus until their salt-and-pepper cords made a skirt around Jesus's heart. Red plaid skirts and corduroys crisscrossed the hall in front of Jesus and his heart.

"The president is dead."

"No, he isn't."

"He's just shot."

"No, he's dead," the skirts and cords said.

We walked home by Gold's Furniture Store with the big gold letters on the front that Stepdad said was full of *ladrones*, crooks; by the Thrifty drug store where Mother got the St. Joseph's children's aspirin; and by the Purina dog food factory where they made Dr. Ross's Dog Food. Only today we didn't feel like singing, so we hummed the jingle we sang every day when we walked past it.

"*Dr. Ross' Dog Food is doggone good, arf*!"

We decided to take the shortcut home through the open-air market. There were baskets of red and yellow onions, tomatoes, tomatillos, garlic, and every kind of chili you could think of. The market was quiet, the cement wet from just being watered. Aproned men at the butcher counter gathered white bloody aprons in their hands, and headscarf–clad women clutched babies to their breasts. They stood around a transistor radio.

"*KWKW, KWKW, te informa primero.*" The KWKW radio jingle rolled out and didn't roll back like it usually did. It spilled out of the radio and ran flat against the wet concrete foundation of the market and laid there like it needed a brush or a mop to move it.

Fish sellers had piled fish onto silver scales and left them there. Shiny heads hung over scale trays, their eyes bald and mouths open.

"*El presidente Kennedy fue asesinado hoy día en Dallas. La primera dama Jaqueline Kennedy escapó danõ,*" the radio announcer said.

My brothers bunched up by the twenty-five-pound bags of beans and rice.

"What did it say? What did it say?" Ted asked. His elbows left dents in the rice sacks when he pushed himself away from them. His straight black hair pointed into a beak in the middle of his forehead, and he was always poking out questions.

"The president got assassinated," I said. "We'd better get home and call Mom."

"What does 'assassinated' mean?" he wanted to know.

I smoothed the red surplice of my uniform and pushed the steel knob for the light to change. "It means he's dead and some-body killed him on purpose," I explained.

I checked the buttons on the side of my uniform and pushed the platinum light changer again.

"Why would somebody want to kill him?" Ted asked.

Ted pecked out questions at me all the way home and up the stairs and to the door. By the time we got there, I'd had enough of Ted and his questions. The door of the fourplex was locked. Mother opened it, her black patent leather purse under her arm.

Mother put her hand over Ted's mouth. "I know, I know," she said, like hushing wouldn't make it so bad. She looked over to see if we were all there. "You kids get inside, and get your uniforms off right away," she instructed.

Mother pulled a Parliament cigarette out of her purse and shifted her purse to her other arm. "Don't ask me why, but I have to go back to work," she said. "Mrs. Elizondo is going to give me a ride."

Her pink cheeks lit up when she lifted the cigarette up to her face for a light.

Mrs. Elizondo's red Chevy pulled up outside.

"I want you kids to stay in the house 'til I get home," Mother said. She walked over to the car. From the window, I could hear her talk to Mrs. Elizondo through the passenger side of the car.

"I'll be right out, Elsa. I've got to get these kids inside. My god, they might be coming after Catholics," she said.

Mother's black patent leather purse flashed sunlight into the house when she walked back up the stairs.

"While I'm gone, remember, stay inside, and before you do your homework, I want you to get your rosaries out to pray a whole rosary for the president's soul."

Mother's pink lips left kiss marks on my brothers' heads. Mother gave me her *you're-in-charge* look. "If anything happens, you call me at work right away, do you hear me?"

Mother closed the front door and locked it behind her. The red Chevy drove off.

We knelt in front of the Virgen de Guadalupe. Her shrine was in a corner of the house in front of a window that was cracked, so it always looked like lightning behind the Virgen when we prayed to her.

Ted sat back on his heels.

"Hail Mary, full of grace, the Lord is with thee . . ."

His rosary folded into the line of his jeans between his closed legs.

We prayed to the Mexican Virgen de Guadalupe in times of crisis, not the Holy Mother.

"Does it count to pray to the Virgen if we pray to her in English?" Ted wanted to know. So many questions.

I held a plastic bead in my hand so I wouldn't lose my place after the first sorrowful mystery. "We've always prayed to the Virgen in English," I replied.

I looked at the Virgen's face. It was the same face—always the same. I didn't know how else to pray to her.

CHAPTER 10

RELICS

My lips twisted up like the salty prunes we got at the Chinese store, three for a nickel on the way home from St. Turibius Catholic School. I chewed the salty pulp off the pit and curled the pit in my tongue, rubbing my tongue against it until the last bit of salt was gone.

Side by side, our schoolgirl uniform skirts rolled up to just above our knees, we walked over cracks, broken bottles, and rusted cans, Ramona taking tiny bites off of her prune. Almost like the prune was going to eat her before she could eat it.

The huge stucco church door was closed to the yellow-hot midafternoon heat. Heat that melted everything around it except the succulents and weeds in the hard dirt outside. Ramona's skinny prune elbow arms and mine pulled straight on the metal circle handle that fell into a metal latch in the middle of the door. The huge arched door dragged against hot cement stairs. Inside, the shiny terra-cotta tile floor was cool, and, except for the light from St. Joseph's window and the red glass candles, it was dark. The air was cool and smelled of burning wax and incense from the high mass the night before. The candles to the Holy Mother had burned into gargoyle shapes in the shadows.

We crossed ourselves in front of the monstrance.

Heaven above and earth below, heart to heart, I've got to go.

Our knees to the kneeler, our butts against the line of the pew in back of us, we sat down.

Ramona took small bites off her prune. "You mean somebody's dead body is locked up in a box behind the altar?" she said.

"Yup, that's what Sister Philadelphia said," I answered.

"No, Sister Filomena," Ramona corrected, still taking small bites of her prune.

"That's what I said. A gnarled-up piece of Turibius is in there in a box for us to pray to."

"I wonder how long he's been in there."

"Well, since he died I guess," I replied.

"How did they know he was a saint when he died? I mean, did they cut a piece off of him right there? Or did they dig him up later, you know, after he went to heaven?"

Prune to her lips, Ramona went back to thinking about the questions. The dark skin of the last part of her prune shriveled off the pit into her mouth.

"Besides, what did he do, you know, I mean, to make him a saint?" she asked. "Did he kill Communists? Or disobey a greedy king?"

"I don't think they had Communists back then," I answered.

"Well, then why are we supposed to pray to him? I wonder what he looks like." Ramona pushed the prune pit around the inside of her cheeks.

"He probably looks like your prune, a tiny, shriveled-up piece of meat stuck to a bone."

"Oooh!"

"Who knows what part of St. Turibius you're eating."

Ramona licked her lips. "Only the good part," she said. "You can have the rest."

Ramona's pit landed in the middle of my red pleated skirt. I straightened the skirt and pulled the pleats flat and sent the pit down the aisle to just in front of the white alabaster communion rail.

Our own offering.

Outside, the large arched doors with the metal rings fell back, metal to metal, into their place. My polyester-cotton shirt stuck to my back, and the sweat rolled down and stopped at the line of my slip. The little white satin bow on Ramona's slip popped up over her buttoned uniform shirt. Our rolled-up red-and-white pleated wool skirts opened and closed over our legs. Hot air blew up against the skin of my thighs, outside, in the heat.

The sun glimmered on the broken-glass-cut diamonds in the dirt.

Step on a crack. Break your mother's back.

Step on a line. Break your mother's spine.

We stepped over cracks and lines across the broken concrete before us. Our feet could only go this way, not that way, as we sang The Dixie Cups' "Chapel of Love."

Ramona's hips and mine hung over our legs like baskets of mango, papaya, and pomegranate, beautiful in color, ripe and carefully cultivated by our parents, a contrast to the ordinary oranges and apples we saw everywhere around us. We only liked pomegranate. The red beads of pomegranate fruit held the danger of permanent red stains on our white blouses. Red and stains and forbidden were why we liked pomegranate.

Mango and papaya were what our parents ate, but we never touched them. Mango and papaya were like the old songs Stepdad played on his record player, sweet and sad, about vengeance in "Venganza, Venganza, Venganza" and cowardly lovers in "Nuestra Cobardía."

We carried our pomegranate, mango, and papaya hips down the block to The Dixie Cups and "The Stroll." Ramona moved over to her side of the sidewalk, and I moved to mine. We made room for Fats Domino.

Our red plaid pleats opened and closed to the two-two beat step of Fats's *"ho-ome,"* and we landed in front of Mrs. Watkins's corner garden. Mrs. Watkins's gate was black wrought iron, shiny in the light. Hers was the cleanest, straightest, and shiniest fence on the block, or any block in the neighborhood. Mrs. Watkins took her clippers to the rosebushes, and to anybody who got too close to her roses. Her roses popped through the black iron gate like birds out of a nest. They hung there, their heads bobbing and mouths open. *Babosas.* The pink roses pushed their way through their metal cage because they could, or because they didn't know better. They couldn't help but be pink, beautiful, and fragrant—they just wanted to be there, fence or no fence.

As we turned the corner of the black metal fence that encased Ms. Watkins's garden, we met two girls with shiny black hair and skin darker than ours. They wore mid-calf jeans over their hips, and their baskets were full of sweet potatoes and yams.

Our wadded-up-at-the-waist, pleated red plaid uniform skirts dangled over our skinny hips. We met them, white shirts to white shirts, tennies to tennies, hair to hair, lips to lips.

"What chu doing to Mrs. Watkins roses?" the girl with a black comb in her hair asked.

"Nothin," I said. "Mrs. Watkins lets anybody touch her roses."

"Spic, don't chu touch Mrs. Watkins roses," the girl with the black comb said.

"Nigger, I will," I said.

"Spic!"

"Nigger!"

The tattoo on my uncle's upper right cheek and the open pores on his reddish-brown face came out of nowhere. The blue-black dot on his face moved into the folds of his skin. Sweat gathered into little rivers over his eyebrows and followed the line down his face from his eyes to his nose to his lips. My back hit cold bricks, and my sweat pushed through the white cotton polyester of my shirt, flimsy against the cool bricks at my back.

My uncle's brown-red face gnarled up to a spit.

"Don't you ever, ever, let me hear you say that word again. Do you hear me?" he said.

My back against the cool bricks, my feet not touching the ground, my head moved up and down and my eyes felt fat with tears.

I saw his lips move but couldn't hear him anymore.

The prune I was saving dropped in the dirt by my feet.

My shirt pulled up out of my skirt, the tips of my white tennies in the dirt, my uncle slowly lowered me. I ran up the stairs. I fell and my knees hit the concrete steps. I pulled my bag and the rest of me up the steps, inside, and sat down on the middle section of mother's aqua, metal-flake sectional. The hot wind blew the plastic flower curtains against my face. The only thing I had to dry my face with was the hot wool of my skirt.

CHAPTER 11

CANASTA

fter work, Mother's ride dropped her at the bus stop at the end of the block. I sat in the front room with my feet resting on the long plank hardwood floor that connected the whole house. My pink metal-flake glasses pushed up against the plastic flower curtain that covered the side window to the street where Mother was coming from. The front window had three faces, one big one to the front and two side faces, one to each side of the street. One side faced the bus that took you to the city, and the other faced the park and the church.

The wooden floor ran like a river under the two big doors that slid into and out of the walls. In the next room on the other side of the sliding doors was the room where a bed went up into a wall. When the bed was up, the wall turned around into a bookcase. At night when Mother and Stepdad slept on the wall bed, the turned-into-the-wall bookcase lived in the closet where my brothers once lit matches and almost burned the house down.

The rooms were mopped and the entire house was clean. The wood went from wet gray to gold again. My hands were red from twisting and squeezing the mop. I pushed them into the pleats of my red school skirt with its hem hanging, another thing to fix, and waited for Mother's slow walk up the long block from the bus stop to the house, the length of the empty lot that was our baseball diamond.

Mother's wide back and shoulders were stuffed under a short black coat. She almost never walked anywhere without being buttoned all the way up, even when it was hot. When she stood in front of our fourplex Mother crossed her arms in front of her, like she didn't want anyone to see her. When people were around she crossed them even tighter with her fists closed so nobody would think it was her fault that men looked at her breasts and said things to her.

On the way home from the bus stop, Mother couldn't fold her arms or ball up her fists because she had to carry things, so she walked with her arms unfolded like her body was somebody else's, not hers. She left her body when she couldn't cover herself. Her brown lunch sack in her hand bounced against her purse.

On the street side of the baseball diamond on the way home from the bus stop there were two stumps of concrete stairs that led up to where houses had once been. Now they were the steps that led to nowhere.

The invisible doors at the top of the stumps opened to a lot full of rocks, glass, dirt, and broken brick. The jagged heels and lips of broken bottles lay everywhere in the dirt. Green 7-Up bottles with white lettering, brown beer bottles, and just plain old torn-label Tokay and Night Train bottles were broken and lay next to each other just out of reach. Broken in ways never to be whole again, here and there, close but not touching. Rusted cans with bands of rippled tin at the top and bottom were folded in half to make rusted points in the folds. Bottle caps, cigarette butts, strips of rubber, broken glass, and the dirt they lay in, all of this was our diamond.

Mother walked her factory shoes past the first stump of stairs. When Mother walked that way, like she was somewhere else, I knew Mother could break up all over me and scatter everywhere like the broken bottles in the diamond, ready to cut you if you fell wrong. Lately she was usually bent over like a rusted can when she walked by the diamond.

I couldn't wait. I rubbed my red hands in the red of my pleated skirt and ran out to meet her as she got to the second stump of stairs to nowhere. Her factory shoes kept moving, and I looked up at her through my pink plastic metal-flake glasses.

"What do you want?" she said.

"Mom, I was waiting for you to come home so I could . . ."

"Why aren't you getting your work done?"

"I did my work, Mom."

"All of it?" she asked.

"Yes."

"Was that you in the window?"

"I wanted to ask you if I could go to a meeting at the CYO about summer camp," I replied.

"I told you to never open that curtain and to stay away from the window, didn't I?" she said.

Mother's flattened grease-spotted lunch bag bounced against her purse when she walked.

"Yes, Mom, but I wasn't sure when you were coming home, and they told us not to be late," I said.

"I get here the same time every day. Now, I told you to stay away from that window. You aren't going anywhere today. You are staying home," she said.

When she shattered like that, it was hard to miss getting stabbed by her flying pieces.

I said nothing and stood there to let her see where she cut me.

"Don't look at me like that," she said. "I don't need any reason to smack the shit out of you."

I learned about wanting and not wanting from Mother's stories about wanting and Canasta.

"When I was fifteen," Mother said, "your grandpa Vidal gave me my first charge account, and I bought my first cashmere sweater to go to the dance at the CY-HI. It was pink and had tiny satin buttons halfway up the back and little pearls like tiny drops on the front. My girlfriend Martha came in the back door of our house with her long, long, black hair all curled up in her hand so I could help her put it up. She had to hide everything she did the night after her sister, your aunt Carmen, ran off with Uncle Joe.

"The night they ran off, it was the one night a month that the Mormons let the Mexicans in Salt Lake use the Terrace Ballroom for a dance. Your uncle Joe was in his uniform, just back from Korea with the rest of the Mexican GIs from Salt Lake and Provo. Your aunt Carmen walked into the dance with her cousins Stella and Rose. They dressed like the Mexican Andrews Sisters. Your aunt Carmen had hips and hair that made men want to throw her over their shoulder in a jitterbug. She was ready.

"Your aunt Carmen didn't go home that night or ever again. The next day, Aunt Carmen's dad and uncles went over to get her. Uncle Joe said she wasn't going back. Said he'd escaped Grandma Mercedes, fought Mormons all his life, and shot Koreans. Carmen was his. Aunt Carmen's dad and uncles left to get the rest of their family. Word got out, and your uncles Shag, Hailo, and Reg went to go round up some of the other guys. When they all left, Uncle Joe and Aunt Carmen borrowed a car and drove to Wendover to get married.

"Carmen's mother never let Martha out of the house again without one of her brothers.

"Your grandpa Vidal said I could charge whatever I wanted, so I got a new pair of Joycees too. Martha brought over a pair of Aunt Carmen's stockings, and we both tried them on with the Joycees. After we put Martha's hair up, I had one more thing to do before going to meet Martha and her brother to go to the dance.

"I had to play and beat your great-grandma Mercedes at a game of Canasta.

"If I won, Great-Grandma Mercedes let me go; if she won, I had to stay home. Every time I won, Grandma Mercedes would make me play another hand. I played again and again until it was almost too late to go to the dance. Then I'd lose to stop playing, and Great-Grandma Mercedes said I had to stay home because I lost," Mother said.

Mother couldn't forgive me for being alive any more than Mercedes could forgive her for being alive.

CHAPTER 12

GORDITAS AND ORANGE PEEL

*S*tepdad got the Union Pacific to transfer him out of Salt Lake to Los Angeles. Mother's family, over three generations in Utah, had learned to deal with the Mormons. But my old-school, first-generation Mexicano stepfather had no stomach for Sugartime Utah and LDS-only racism.

It was years before we saw Grandma Mary again. By that time, Mother had successfully sued my great-grandmother Mercedes for custody of me. Mother had been seventeen, Mexican, and unwed in 1950s Utah when I was born. She gave me up to Great-Grandma Mercedes to raise and got me back before we moved to LA.

By the time we moved to LA, Grandma Mary and her *comadres* no longer shut down Salt Lake City taverns, and her visits to LA were longer and more frequent. She spent her time between kitchens in Salt Lake and LA perfecting the recipes that made our family's Salt Lake City Mexican restaurants famous during the 1930s, '40s, and '50s.

At eleven years of age, I was still running in a pack with my brothers when the news came that Grandma Mary was coming for a visit.

In the days before she arrived, Mother undertook a massive kitchen cleaning operation. Beginning with the stove, every inch, every crevice of tile and linoleum, enamel, and Formica was stripped of dirt and scrubbed down to near below the paint and finish.

A bleached-out wooden pole with a rusted clamp bolted on the top was our mop. Strips of faded beach towels and worn-out school blouses were fed into the open rusted mop clamp head. Mother pulled the metal clamp down shut over the threadbare Tweety Bird towel strips and leaned the mop up against a new jug of Clorox, Mr. Clean, a silver-sealed Ajax can, and shiny metallic rust pot scrubbers.

"This kitchen's got to be spic and span," Mother said.

The kitchen was full of Grandma and cleaning still lifes. Cleaning products were arranged in groups of two or three in compositions of rusted metallic pot scrubbers, new tall blue Ajax cans, short square orange Spic and Span boxes, rag mops, buckets, and brushes.

Mother hit the mop pole on the floor like a spear until my spell was broken.

"My mother was what she was," she said, hitting the floor again. "She was what she was, but she always kept a clean kitchen. And whatever she was, she was my mother," Mother said.

On the night before Grandma's visit, we were all so sick with excitement that we couldn't sleep. We sat on our beds and made cutouts for her from the blue triangular foil inserts that Mother brought home from the envelope factory.

The next day, we went to pick her up from the train station. We ran as we did, in a pack behind our mother. The red-top, yellow–long body of the Union Pacific piled up car by car behind Grandma's train.

Grandma stood on the wooden platform just outside the ceiling-high glass doors that opened to Union Station. Her pink compact open, she brushed pink cheeks on her small brown face.

A cigarette balanced between her lips, and her compact mirror flashed broken light over us like a Morse code.

I don't know how I knew what I knew about her. Maybe it was the look on Mother's face, the face of a woman who, as a child, had seen Grandma passed out on a city bus bench from a school bus window. The face of a woman who, time after time, waited for each visit to be different. This time there would be no fork in the turkey stuffing, no man on the back porch, and no more hidden flasks.

This time there would only be Grandma's very best red mole, hog's head tamales, hot chocolate *atole*, syrup-dipped orange peel *capirotada*, and enough buttery gorditas for the whole neighborhood.

When Grandma stepped off the platform, we ran to her; we made our circle around her, the backs of our hands touching. We never held each other's hands or touched each other in any way. Only when Grandma visited did we get close enough to smell our smell of city sweat through striped cotton T-shirts. Close in, around her, blue foil trees in hand, we shared our love for her, and by default, our love for each other. Mother waited in the doorway of the LA station while we circled Grandma.

Grandma smiled that smile you smile with a cigarette in your mouth, half-open, half-closed. She gathered spit between her thumb and forefinger and doused the red-lit tip of her cigarette with her fingers to put an end to it, midway. She tamped the red ember into a spit-ash crust and slid it next to the fresh white sticks in the bull's-eye pack. The pack in her purse, she pressed the black-ink-on-blue seal back into place and pulled out a pack of Black Jack and gave us each a stick of licorice gum. She touched our faces and reached over to kiss us, her red lips smelling of gin, Sen-Sen, and Lucky Strikes.

"Don't forget to get all those boxes," she said.

With the shiny black strap of her purse in the crook of her arm, her short shadow stood stiff over the station wagon. The bags, boxes, and valises were loaded on top of the wagon, and the rest of us settled into the back of the Chevy. In the second seat behind my stepdad, Grandma's arm draped over the gold clip that shut her purse. She unbuttoned the tiny blue rose button on her blouse, closed her eyes, and leaned up against the car door.

The tiny black moles on her cheek made a crescent that moved up and down on her face all the way home, past the naked Styrofoam mannequins in Garment District windows, past the rolled-down loading dock doors, and past the concrete banks that cradled the puddle that was the LA River. Her feet just touching the car floor behind Stepdad, she was little—too little for a woman who could shut down all the taverns in Salt Lake City if she had to.

From her boxes that we'd stacked on the kitchen table, one by one, Grandma unpacked folded packets of anise seed, ground nutmeg, dried shrimp, cinnamon sticks, several kinds of chilies, a dozen individually wrapped pie tart tins, her rolling pin, a marble slab, cooking shears, an *atole* wand, and more.

On baking days, we stood around the yellow Formica to watch her.

"Commere," she said.

She pressed our fingers into the dough around the edges of individual pie pans to teach us how to flute them. Our fingers in the dough, we pushed and pinched until all the flutes were even. With kitchen scissors, she cut leaves out of the leftover dough and laid them in nine different patterns on each of our pies, one for each of us.

For fruit pies, she cut dough strips and showed us how to lay them one over the other into a lattice crust. Her masterpiece was peach pie. Piles and piles of peaches were peeled, sliced, and layered under a thick blanket crust. Rock sugar was strewn over the top.

For Mother, Grandma baked a special yam pie with browned marshmallows all over the top of it. Only Mother liked that Utah pie. Each year we were required to taste it, a finger's full in our mouths. Mother happily ate the rest of the finger-gauged pie.

Our faces together pressed up to the oven window, we took turns, three at a time, to watch the browning dough leaves on our potpies. We found ourselves once more sharing our love for pies, for Grandma, and by default, for each other.

In the mornings, a large pot of thick corn gruel laced with chocolate was ladled into clay cups. We sat around the table with Grandma to drink the corn gruel that was so hot that it burned our lips.

"Slowly. Drink it slowly," she said.

After a few days, the corn and the chocolate made a flavor so sweet and savory that the burning didn't matter. On those mornings, Grandma took her *atole* with us, her red lips on the clay rim cup.

"This is what we drank at the fire every morning at labor camps in Utah, when I was a little girl."

The clay cup smell was warm, not like the cool clay smell of summer water.

"And around the fire, where I played with your mother like she was a doll," she added.

After school, Grandma waited for us with thick gorditas in hand. Slabs of melted butter rolled down the sides of our hands. Through the swing gate and up our red steps, our friends lined up for theirs. The worst threat to anybody on our block was to be cut off from our grandma Mary's thick hot corn gorditas.

When the food was all cooked and put away, Grandma took out her playing cards and showed us how to play solitaire. King, queen, jack, spades, hearts, one on top of another we learned to calculate play. She taught us to evaluate rank, establish order, and end play when the game was over. As we sat next to her, her red lips and coffee breath against our faces, she'd say:

"The worst thing you can do is skip a play."

"It does you no good to cheat yourself."

"Nobody knows but you. But a lie is still a lie."

"Worst of all, it kills the game."

CHAPTER 13

SAINT CHRISTOPHER

We never met Stepdad's dad, but he was always around. We knew his name, but it was never spoken. It was the same name as Stepdad's, Antonio Martinez. It was his given name; Stepdad was Ozuna on his mother's side. Antonio Martinez Sr. gave his name to Stepdad when Stepdad was born even though he wasn't married to Stepdad's mother. Then later, Antonio Sr. gave his name, the same first name, to the son born to the woman he did marry. He gave it away like he hadn't already given it to Stepdad. Like Stepdad wasn't born first. Like he didn't exist. Like it didn't matter.

Everywhere he went, Stepdad was the doubt created by his naming. There but not there. Seen but not seen. Named and unnamed. Documented and undocumented.

One day when we were on the way home from school in the car with Stepdad, we decided to break it to him: the saint on his dashboard wasn't really a saint after all, and Father at school said that we didn't need to pray to Saint Christopher anymore.

Stepdad stared out the window. What happened to all those prayers, Stepdad wanted to know, and what happened to all the journeys that had been taken or might have been taken but for prayers to the fictitious saint? Stepdad was on a roll, on one of his favorite subjects, the Catholic Church, and the Catholic Church in Mexico in particular.

That's when Saint Christopher became our patron saint. Stepdad liked him because Saint Christopher was the saint who never existed. He was like us in that way. There but not there.

At bedtime, when Mother thought he was telling us about Dick and Jane and Yankee Doodle, Stepdad told us bedtime stories about his own dead babies, the Mexican dead babies.

"There were dead babies hidden in churches all over Mexico. During the revolution, they found little skeletons wrapped up in blankets and hidden in the walls in basilicas bigger than all the churches in Rome," Stepdad said.

"That's where the Limbo babies are," my brother whispered. "In a little room in the cellars at Our Lady of Guadalupe." Limbo babies were always a fascination for Catholic kids. They were the babies who were born but not yet baptized before they died. Because they weren't baptized they couldn't get to heaven, so their souls roamed aimlessly in the universe, never to rest.

On another night, we heard about all the gold. The Church had lots of gold. There were rooms of gold, gold bricks, gold and silver coins in velvet bags. That's why priests and nuns wore long skirts, Stepdad said. So they could carry around their bags of gold and nobody would know. During the revolution, when people were hungry and dying in the street, the Church bought ornaments for their altars, he said.

We couldn't wait for bedtime and wiped *pan dulce* crumbs off our faces so we could get into our pajamas and get to bed. In Stepdad's world, it was practically forbidden to go to bed without "esneck," our snack of sweet bread, *pan dulce,* and milk. If we had fallen asleep, he would wake us. The piggies were our favorite in the vast array of Mexican breads to choose from— *novias* (brides), *elotes* (corn), *conchas* (shells)—each bread with a regional story that changed with the teller.

Crumbs dusted off, we climbed into bed. When Stepdad told bedtime stories, we had heroes better than Superman. We had Cuauhtémoc. Cuauhtémoc was the bravest Aztec in all of Mexico. When Moctezuma, who was weak, got tricked by the evil *Gachupines* (Spaniards) into giving up most of Mexico's gold and jewels, it was Cuauhtémoc who hid the rest of the treasure and organized an army to fight back. When the Spaniards caught him, they demanded the treasure and burned his feet to make him tell. They tied him up and built a fire and burned his feet slowly, until he had no feet. He still wouldn't tell, so they killed him. The Spaniards never got the treasure. Stepdad said the treasure was still out there, somewhere, waiting to be found. Cuauhtémoc's mythic treasure and his burning feet were all I could think about. A leader's willingness to suffer and die to protect his people.

The next night, piled up on the one bed we all slept on, we learned about Los Niños Héroes de Chapultepec, the cadets who wrapped themselves in the Mexican flag and flung themselves off a cliff to avoid the surrender of the flag.

Then came the night he told us about the heads on the poles. It was during a bad, bad time in Mexico that Stepdad called the *Porfiriato*, when the people were so hungry, they had no bread, and the rich lived in palaces. Pancho Villa and his soldiers came to the towns where the people were hungry and told the greedy merchants to lower their prices so the people could afford to buy bread. He gave the merchants a week to make their changes. When he came back, some had lowered their prices and others had not. Those who had not were hung. Their heads were chopped off and stuck on poles for all the town to see. Nobody took their heads down; they stayed up on the poles until they rotted away. Rotted heads, eyes bulging, being picked at by vultures.

When he wasn't telling bedtime stories, Stepdad held captive audience meetings with us to discuss the intricacies of Church canon or Mexican history. His six-pack of Budweiser at the ready, we'd sometimes have to sit and listen for hours.

He'd especially drink during visits from Antonio Sr., who we never saw but who could show up anytime and anywhere. Like when we went to school on parents' night or when we brought our schoolbooks home, Antonio Sr. was there to remind Stepdad that he was uneducated and nothing more than a common laborer. That Stepdad's brother, the other Antonio, was an engineer, and the third brother was a lawyer.

Antonio Sr. made special visits when we brought home our Spanish books.

"*Pinches Gachupines*," Stepdad said, his bad word for Spaniards, when we made the mistake of bringing home our *Spanish Today* textbook with its "*Holas*" and "*Qué tals*" in it. Our Spanish books always had pictures of Spain and Argentina in them, never Mexico, Stepdad pointed out. Castilian gates opened to brick terraces in our Spanish book, and Buenos Aires was pictured as a cosmopolitan city near a blue ocean bay.

We knew we were in for a long session when Stepdad sat us down for the day's lecture on the fine points of Spanish diction, the proper Mexican way.

CHAPTER 14

EGGS, TORTILLAS,

AND REFRIED BEANS

Our phone was turned off again, and I had to go to the Garcias' at the corner to call the police. I walked down the chipped and faded red front concrete steps, lifted the metal latch on the gate, closed the chain-link gate behind me, and walked the length of the ivy-covered fence past the Chinese house. We called it the Chinese house because elderly Chinese bachelors lived there. They trimmed their roses and swept and watered their sidewalk early in the morning before anybody else got up. We loved their roses and their clean, wet sidewalk as much as they did, so we never drew hopscotches in front of their house or ran sticks against their fence or threw stuff in their yard.

We only saw them when they gave things away.

They gave me a very old wooden RCA radio with a decal of a Dalmatian sitting next to a Victrola on it. The radio had large dials, and brown cloth stretched over the speakers. It took a while to get the radio going because the tubes were old and dusty. The tube light lit low then beamed red, cracking when the tubes got warm and the radio was on.

I loved the stories in the songs on *Huggy Boy's Golden Oldies* show, songs about finding work, mothers-in-law and sitting in the park waiting for someone.

On special nights when the signal was right, we could get Wolfman Jack from Ensenada.

"Are you naked?" he'd ask a caller in a low voice.

"Yes, Wolfman," the caller said. "Just for you."

The Wolfman would send out a lone wolf howl throughout the airwaves.

"I want to make a dedication," the caller said.

The song was to "Flaco," "Smiley," or "Chuy," and was either "Daddy's Home," or "The Town I Live In," the early McKinley Mitchell version, or "Angel Baby." On rare occasions someone would request a real oldie like "Does Your Mama Know About Me?" The dedications were stories inside the stories of the songs about longing, breakups, betrayal, and just sappy love.

The Garcias' house was next to the Chinese house. It was on the corner of the block that turned down the hill. The hill held up a whole block of houses. Our bungalow was on a ridge, and our backyard was the slope of the hill below. The Garcias' corner house went all the way down the hill like a train. Rooms had been added on to make room for all the Garcia kids. At ten, they had one more kid than we did. Their house looked like a set of boxcars. Each stucco block addition was a different color. Not bright, bright colors but pastel colors of yellow, pink, and aqua. Alongside the hill outside each of the new rooms, there were tiny red patios with pink geraniums, potted trees, and red-and-green coleuses tucked in everywhere.

I knocked on the screen door of the first boxcar room, the main house. Mrs. Garcia was breastfeeding the new baby. Mrs. Garcia's mother-in-law, the other Mrs. Garcia, walked up the hill from the bus stop. Home from work, she got to the door when

I did. The Garcia kids called their grandma Nana, and we did too. Nana wore a business suit and high heels. She held the door open for me with her elbow so Mrs. Garcia, the baby's mother, didn't have to get up to answer the door. Nana put her black patent leather purse down by the baby table and walked over to get the baby. She sat in a chair by the geraniums, unbuttoned her blouse, slid her lace slip strap over her shoulder, lifted her bra, and put the baby to her breast.

"Come in, come in," Mrs. Garcia, the baby's mother, said.

She folded the bumpy blue-striped receiving blanket she'd used to cover herself when she was nursing and put it with a stack of cloth diapers on the baby table next to Nana's patent leather purse.

I knew where the black rotary-dial phone was. I had been there to use it before. It was on top of the red Manteca Cudahy cans piled in the corner of the kitchen that Mr. Garcia got from the slaughterhouse where he worked.

I picked up the heavy metal telephone handle and dialed O. The cutout metal dial face moved slowly over all the numbers from 1 to O.

"Operator, please, send the police," I said into the phone receiver.

"My father is killing my mother."

"Yes, you've been here before."

"Yes."

"Yes, Fresno and Garnet."

I put the phone down.

In the next room, Nana lifted the baby to her shoulder and smoothed its back until it burped. The baby's black hair poked up into the air and landed with its head against the white diaper on her shoulder. Nana closed her blouse and gave the baby to Mrs. Garcia. They both reached over the baby table to change the baby. I left when their backs were turned.

"Thank you, Mrs. Garcia," I said, and walked to the front

door. Mrs. Garcia looked up with a ducky safety pin like Mother's in her mouth.

I walked past the Chinese house. My radio was on, and I could hear it though the screened window. "I'm on the Outside (Looking In)," by Little Anthony and the Imperials, was playing.

All the Fresno Street kids from down the block were hanging out on the fence when I got there. Medi, his dogs, and some of the Dakota Street kids were there too.

The door to the house was open. Mother was on the living room side of the open doorway. Her face was red and her lip was bleeding.

Stepdad was on the porch. His shirt was torn, and he had scratch marks across his back.

Mother wiped blood off her lip. "You goddamn son of a bitch," she said.

The police turned the corner up the hill by the Garcias' house.

The kids bunched up around the hinged metal gate. I watched from inside through the bay window. Medi's dog pulled against the leather strap around his neck.

"The police are coming," one of the kids said.

Stepdad walked backward down the top two red steps. "You were nothing but a whore when I met you," he said.

Mother threw the rest of his shirt at him. "And you were nothing but a goddamn pimp," she said.

A pimp? What is a pimp? There was nobody to ask. I'd have to wait 'til Monday to see if it was in Sister Jerome's giant dictionary.

Whatever it was, Stepdad froze.

The police got out of the black-and-white.

"To protect and to serve," was written in a gold seal on the car door. The car door swung open and cut into the dirt. A nightstick hit the curb.

Stepdad walked backward down the last two steps still facing Mother and then turned away from her. The lines on his back were bleeding.

Mother walked out of the doorway and onto the porch. Her eye was swollen shut.

"Go ahead and run, you coward. Now that the police are coming," Mother said.

An officer with a buzz cut walked through the gate.

"Mr. Martinez, can we talk to you?" he said.

Stepdad picked up a jacket off the porch and walked toward the gate.

"Mr. Martinez," he repeated.

Stepdad checked his jacket pocket. He rubbed his hands against his thighs over his pockets to feel for keys like he did when he went to work.

The police officer with the buzz cut took another step inside the gate toward Stepdad.

"Mr. Martinez, have you got somewhere else to go?"

Stepdad shook his jacket. No keys.

"Women wear the pants in this country," Stepdad said.

The police officer took another step into the yard.

"Just take a walk, Mr. Martinez, and cool off," he said.

"Whaddyou mean? This is my house, I work hard for it," Stepdad said. He opened his palms in a plea.

Mother walked out of the doorway and onto the porch. She pulled her torn blouse together and crossed her arms over her bosom. "And don't come back, you asshole," she said.

The officer pushed open the gate. "Ma'am, can I have you go inside?" he asked.

Stepdad passed the officer on the steps. "See what I mean?" he said.

Stepdad threw his jacket over his back and walked out of the gate and down the street. Stepdad never left the house without his keys, and he never walked anywhere.

Mother took a step down the stairs and watched him go down the street. His jacket bounced off his back like he was skipping down the sidewalk. He didn't look back.

The officer stepped back and closed the gate.

"Now you kids go home," he said.

He walked toward the kids with his hand opened to shoo them away.

In the morning, Stepdad showed up. His back was red. The blood on his back had dried into parallel curved lines.

He walked to the back sink where the Tweety Bird towel was hanging on the rack. He made a face when he reached his scratched shoulder under the water. I watched from the doorway.

"*¿Ivan y venian, donde esta tu madre?*" he said. *Where is your mother?*

"She's in the kitchen," I said.

"*Dile qu tego hambre,*" he said. *Tell her I'm hungry.*

He rubbed Tweety Bird's big head against the scratches on his back. I stared at his back. I wanted to be Tweety and say what I saw. I didn't.

Stepdad pulled the towel over his head. I was still standing there.

Finally, Tweety back on the nail, he said, "*Cicatrices de batalla.*" *Battle scars.*

I didn't need to tell Mother he wanted breakfast; she was already cooking it. This was the choreography of their marriage, the final act of the three-act play that was their marriage over thirty years. Stepdad entered the kitchen and sat down to eat like he had just come back from the store with the milk. His scratches were cured on his back in the light that came through the clothes-line window like the bacon Mother placed on his plate next to the eggs she fried for him. Mother's eye was covered in makeup.

They sat together at the kitchen table by the window under the Union Pacific Railroad calendar. Stepdad dug his singed tortilla into his beans. Mother broke the egg yolk with the other half of Stepdad's tortilla. Stepdad poured coffee for Mother. Mother got up to heat him another tortilla.

CHAPTER 15

I WAS GOING TO TELL YOU

Grandma Mary's gin-and-Pall-Mall breath was the thing I remembered, along with her Morse code compact that sent signals for clues to her secrets. Clues that I held on to. Clues that made everything else I learned about her, and later about me, true. Grandma at the train station, red eyed and red lipped with her gin-and-Pall-Mall breath, opened the door to all the other secrets in my family. Secrets my mother wouldn't let us hear because if you opened one you would have to open them all.

The thing about secrets is that they don't want to be secrets. They want to be told.

My parents kept a black box in the little closet in the one official bedroom in the bungalow where we found the Hermanas Cortez 78s when we moved in. Official, because the house was a one-bedroom house when we bought it. There were eight of us kids at the time, so Stepdad constructed a makeshift add-on to the back of the house where the boys slept. Stepdad's study was my parent's flat-no-headboard bed in the middle of the official bedroom by the closet where the Hermanas Cortez waited until we found them.

The bed was covered with a starburst quilt that Grandma Jenny, Stepdad's mother, made for him out of scraps that Mother dumpster-dived for in the Garment District. My mother hated that starburst quilt pattern. Stepdad's mother knew only one quilt pattern, so Mother hated all her quilts. When we moved into that house Stepdad hung a picture of the Virgen de Guadalupe over their bed. Years later, when Mother converted to a religion that celebrated no holidays and worshipped no idols, Stepdad moved the Virgen to his side of the bed.

During office hours Stepdad knelt over the side of the bed, his work boots airing by the window. He flipped open the silver latch on the black box so it opened to the hinge at the bottom like a toolbox. The box opened to layers of trays that unfolded accordion style over the starburst orange-and-yellow polyester quilt pattern.

When he had family business to transact or documents to look over, Stepdad closed the bedroom door partway. He opened it only enough so you could see his boots under the window, his knees on the carpet, and his elbows at the edge of the bed like he was praying.

I was in the closet one day to see if there was more stuff to go with the Hermanas Cortez 78s. I wanted to see if there was an album cover with a picture of them on it, like Los Tres Ases: three men in slick black suits with pencil-thin mustaches with guitars in hand sitting around a table with three Aces in a circle and songs on the back jacket with titles like "No Me Platiques Ya," "Jacaranda," and "Sabor a Mí." But there was no album cover for the Las Hermanas Cortez. No way to see what they looked like. No way to see if they wore box-cut dresses that pushed their cleavage up to the black satin line across the top of their bosoms. Black satin dresses that shined over smooth hips. Satin hips and glittering earrings that hung like mini-chandeliers against the black sleeveless satin straps. And high heels that sculpted curves into brown skin.

There were no pictures, only Stepdad's black box. I flipped open the silver latch and unfolded the accordion trays. In the bottom tray, there was a half-sheet document with a black border around it. It said "Birth Certificate" at the top and had the embossed seal of the State of Utah Vital Statistics Department at the bottom. It had my name on it and a box with a check next to it that said "girl," another checked box that said "live birth." By race, there was a box for white. "Non-white" was typed in on the line under the box for white. My mother's name was handwritten on the line for mother. The line for father was blank. When I first held my birth certificate, I knew I was holding on to something I wasn't supposed to have. Something I wasn't supposed to see or officially know. The embossed seal felt like braille and looked like embroidery seed stitches in a circle pattern. I turned it over to feel the embossing in reverse. I held the birth certificate up to the light of the little window in the closet and shook the document, hoping something would fall out it. A chandelier earring from the Hermanas Cortez, maybe, or a clue to who my dad was. But there was nothing, so I put it away.

I was sitting on a bed in the dining room right outside the kitchen where I sometimes slept. There in the dim light with my embroidery hoop I was hoping to find the stitches my tía Chia left for me. There was little light and I didn't have my glasses on, so I held the linen right up to my nose.

"Wha summatta, you bline?" my stepfather said to me on his way to the kitchen to continue his new fight with Mother.

A coffee pot had already landed on the kitchen wall and slid down, coffee grounds splayed with steam against the just-washed-down wall. The little glass globe on the top of the silver metal coffee pot rolled over to the corner where the mousetraps were and snapped one of them.

He stood in the doorway between the kitchen and dining room and yelled at me.

"Get in here!" he said to me. "It's time for you to know. You are not my daughter."

When the coffee pot came flying, Mother had moved herself around the stove to finish the eggs she was frying.

"You your mother's bastard," he said.

I held on to embroidery hoop and pressed the little bird stitches Tía drew for me.

Mother turned off the stove.

"Leave her alone, you chickenshit son of a bitch," Mother said.

Her tough-eyed frame cracked. Her lip softened.

"If you want to fight with me, fight with me, you asshole," she said.

Mother put her spatula under the fried egg to lift it out of the grease and led me out of the kitchen, her hand on my shoulder.

"Leave her out of it, you asshole!" she called out to him from the dining room. She sat me on the bed that was in the dining room where I had been working on my embroidery.

"I'm so sorry you had to find out like this," she said. "I was going to tell you when you were older and could understand. I am so sorry, mija. I am so sorry."

Her lips quivered, and tears came down her face. I gripped my hoop on my lap, looking up at her and not saying anything. It was one of the few times I remember her ever crying and saying she was sorry.

CHAPTER 16

THE RING

The concrete patio outside the kitchen window of our house looked over the back of the block behind us, the empty lot, the Chinese house next door, the houses on the next two blocks, the streets up and down the hill below us, and the clothesline. The clothesline rope hung from a pulley on a pole outside of the kitchen window at the top of our hill. It was connected to a pole with a pulley on it at the other end, at the bottom of our hill. Legs standing and shirts pinched at the collar, our pants and shirts moved across the parallel clothesline in Hully Gully, one arm length at a time over the backyard dirt.

I hung clothes out the kitchen window from a silver two-handled bucket full of wet, heavy jeans. The clothesline rope burned my hands with each pull that sent more empty cloth body parts down the line. Our clothes hung like headless scarecrows, twisted and turned by the wind or stiff and still under the baking sun.

You couldn't get to our patio from the kitchen. You had to go to the back door, past the pigeon coop, and all the way around the house. The patio was a concrete slab held up by wooden pillars in concrete. Because it was on a hill, the whole slab made a terrace. Only wooden railings that any kid could fall under kept you from falling off the edge to the Chinese house's concrete driveway fifty feet below.

There were never parties on the terrace or barbeques or celebrations with relatives. The patio would have been perfect for such parties, but we never had them. There were no flowers of any kind. No one quietly sipped *licuados* of watermelon juice or *agua de Jamaica* by the shade of the house. The patio never went from being much more than hot concrete, unforgiving to fall on and empty, wasted space. It was like us in that way, just out of reach, never realizing its beauty, only the brutality of hard surfaces and the fear of falling off the edge.

It was on the patio where the parties and flowers never were that Stepdad built his portable boxing ring. Ropes wrapped around poles that were filled by cement-filled tires. Around the four poles, twine looped into two parallel lines. At opposite corners of two of the poles, Stepdad hung a pair of red boxing gloves. The gloves burned shiny in the hot sunlight. The red Naugahyde was soft and hung ready. The red gloves hugged the poles, almost touching the buckets below that served as seats for the boxers.

Saturday was boxing day and laundry day. Stepdad wore his sleeveless ribbed cotton tank top with the holes in it and his ringmaster whistle around his neck. Stepdad's medic kit consisted of a rusted bucket of water and ice with a faded towel draped over the top.

Stepdad's rules were simple: no kicking, no biting, no hitting below the belt, whatever started in the ring ended in the ring, and only three minutes per round, no matter what.

Stepdad never let girls in the ring even though I was the oldest and had had more real fights than my seven brothers had. Now that my brothers were learning to box, they didn't need me to beat people up anymore. Not like when we first moved to California.

The boys showed up with their shirts off.

I had to wear a bra under my shirt because Mother said I'd started to develop. I didn't want to develop. I had to wear straps around my chest and straps around my waist to hold up bulky napkins that wadded up between my legs. Saturday was ropes. Ropes around my chest, ropes of laundry, and ropes in the ring.

On this afternoon the patio concrete was really hot, and sweat beaded rivers down our faces. The boxers and ringside spectators leaned against the house in the shade under the iodine bottle Stepdad kept on the window ledge. The boxers matched up. Everybody knew it was fair for Ted to fight Hector and for Jimmy to fight Alvaro. The only person who didn't have a match was Eddie Osorio. Making Eddie cry was sport, but it got you in trouble. Nobody wanted to fight Eddie, because if he went home crying, his mother would come.

Ted and Hector got into the ring. Ted's eyes were dark, and his skin the deepest brown it got all summer. *Mosca en leche,* Stepdad called him. Against the white of our house, he did look like a fly in milk as he lighted his skinny body in the ring. His straight black hair shined and poked out like porcupine quills.

Hector's hair was wavy and brown. It fell over his right eye, and Stepdad liked to call him Veronica Lake. Hector tied a red bandanna around his head to keep his hair out of his eyes. He was *guero*, light-skinned, like his mother, and had dead skin on his shoulders from his last sunburn. He was tall for his age and spoke in three-word sentences that ended with the sound of O.

"Who said so? I don't know. I gotta go."

Stepdad rang the bell, a hammer against a cracked cast-iron skillet that hung from a nail on the side of the house. Ted and Hector danced around the ring for the first minute. Hector wore high-top black Converse with no socks and his red cotton gym trunks. Ted's blue-striped undershorts poked up over his black cutoffs. Ted's low-top tennies had the labels cut out of them. Mother got our tennies at the secondhand shop from the bin where you had to match up the sizes of the single laceless shoes that had tongues flapping and wrapping around each other. Sometimes there were no exact matches, so we had to wear a blue shoe and a black shoe or a shoe one size bigger than the other. We called the big shoe our clown foot. Ted's clown foot curled rubber up over his toes.

Hector threw a punch at Ted. Ted blocked it and threw another one at Hector. That one landed. Hector's jaw flew up, then landed back in place. Hector's square shoulders opened like butterfly wings and he rushed Ted, landing one of three jabs on Ted's right cheek, just under his eye. Ted moved back, faked a right, and almost landed a left on Hector's jaw. Hector blocked the jab and pushed Ted away.

Stepdad slammed the pan. The round was over.

Stepdad stepped into the middle of the ring and held both Ted's and Hector's hands up. Nobody won. It was a draw. Ted's eye was red from the punch he took.

"*Muy macho*," Stepdad said to Ted.

Stepdad poured water over Ted's head. Ted's wet black hair went flat against the side of his face. Stepdad pulled off his other glove and threw a piece of a towel around Ted's neck.

"*Ivan y venian, ve dile a tu madre que nos de mas agua*," Stepdad said. "Ivan y venian" was the nickname Stepdad made up for me because he could never say "Yvonne." Going and coming, coming and going, I was tired of being the water girl, but I went inside to get more.

I grabbed the yellow-top plastic pitcher of water with my fists and carried it to the back door.

"What are you doing outside?" Mother said in her *I-don't-care-what-the-answer-is* voice. Mother wore her Saturday dress, a faded seersucker print from the Sears basement sale. The buttons were popped off, and Mother held it together with safety pins. "Get up there and finish hanging up these pants."

I took the pitcher out to Stepdad and went back to the clothesline. I hung my brothers' pants back-to-back on the line the length of our backyard. Mother pulled more pants through the ringer washer. They came out knife-edged flat and steamed slither snakes into the cold rinse water. Mother lifted the pants out of the rinse water and rolled them back over the wringer to squeeze out the rest of the dirt, then put them onto a pile in the silver bucket for me to shake out and hang.

I pulled the clothesline in and leaned over it to watch Eddie Osorio get into the ring with a bully named Edgar Velazquez. When Stepdad let Edgar into the ring, Edgar didn't box, he slugged.

I pulled myself closer to the line and pulled the wet, heavy jeans out of the laundry tub. The wooden metal-spring clothes-pins opened like the crow's beaks in the park and wouldn't close all the way over the thick denim waistbands. The clothespins hung over the wet jeans like something was stuck in their beaks. I opened three clothespins on the dripping jeans and pulled the line on the pulley to push the jeans into the air over the backyard, hoping they didn't fall a hundred feet into the dirt. I moved the pants down the line with the bird's beaks clothespins open. The clothespins bumped and gagged for the whole neighborhood to see. With each pull of the line, it got heavier and hung lower. From the clothesline window, I had a ringside seat to the patio.

Eddie stood at one corner of the ring. He wore glasses that had a strap around the back of his head that his mother made him wear so he wouldn't lose them. His glasses were so thick that they looked like goggles with the strap on. Eddie hung his glasses on the pole over the bucket where the gloves used to be.

Eddie moved his head around like a blind musician, trying to hear what he couldn't see. Stepdad pulled Eddie's open-fisted glove close to him, toward the hole in the middle of Stepdad's coach tank top. The red glove touched the hair on Stepdad's chest. Stepdad leaned into Eddie to talk to him like he was giving Eddie a blessing. He tied Eddie's gloves tight and pulled them into the middle of the ring. Eddie used his elbows to keep his shorts up. He was in.

Stepdad walked over to the opposite corner of the ring and pulled the laces on Edgar's gloves. He held his hands up flat to Edgar so Edgar could make practice punches.

"Remember," Stepdad said, "you are supposed to box, not fight. No slugging or you are out, got it? Out for good."

Edgar moved his gloves in front of him like he knew what he was supposed to do.

Stepdad hit the pan.

Eddie lifted his gloves in a straight line over his head, bent over, lowered his arms like an airplane, and dove for Edgar. Edgar moved out of the way, and Stepdad caught Eddie and stood him up.

"You are not a toro. This is not a bullring. *Usa tus manos, no tu cabeza.*"

"Okay, Mr. Martinez," Eddie said. "Use my hands, not my head," he repeated. His gloves moved in circles, big red globes around his head.

Edgar moved to the middle of the ring and waved an imaginary matador's cloth in front of Eddie.

"Eddie, you can get out anytime," Stepdad said.

"It's okay, Mr. Martinez," he said. "Use my hands, not my head."

Eddie went back to the middle of the concrete ring.

Eddie moved in with his fists in front of him, like he was trying to be Floyd Patterson.

He lifted his arm and rolled it around like a big windup clock and took off after Edgar. When Eddie's punch landed, Edgar's head bounced off the ropes. Edgar got off the ropes and went after Eddie like he was the bull. Eddie dodged him. Edgar slammed into the ropes and almost knocked the ring over. The concrete tires wobbled. Stepdad hit the pan. It was all over.

Stepdad held Eddie's hand up.

"That was not boxing, Eddie, but sometimes the most important thing is just to get into the ring," Stepdad said.

Stepdad poured water over Edgar.

"Nice moves, Edgar. We are going to have to find you a toro."

Nobody ever said anything to Eddie after that. Nobody ever made fun of him, and nobody ever told his mother that Eddie almost knocked out the biggest bully on the block.

WHEN EVERYONE WAS GONE THE RING ropes hung low like jump ropes held end to end by the rolled-in-concrete poles. I stepped over the rope and lifted the gloves off the pole. With my teeth, I pulled tight on the crisscross laces that went through the middle of the palm side of the glove. My fingers were squeezed together inside the glove, and the gloves buried my hands like fat cushions. I knocked a boxing ring pole back and forth in the cement tire. One time, then another, the pole hit my fist and I sent it back. I boxed until the laces got loose, then pulled them tight again with my teeth.

Everlast, the label on my gloves said. *Everlast.*

CHAPTER 17

OLGA'S SHOP

The fake-wood-panel Ford's butt hung low, its tires nearly flat under the weight of us, three to a window in the back and two with the baby between us in the middle behind our parents. The no-money-down, five-year-payment-plan windows never rolled all the way down. Hot air and Stepdad's cigarette smoke burned holes in our noses. My brothers sat upright, their legs folded, their backs against the station wagon side windows. Everywhere there were bags and sacks wherever they could fit under the seats and underfoot.

Stepdad always got a haircut and had his mustache trimmed before we drove the two hundred miles south to Tía Vicki's. Mother sat next to him in front, but never close enough to touch him or do any more than answer his questions.

"Margara," he said to her in that way she hated, the common Mexican way of distorting her given name, Margaret, to make it sound big and fat. Stepdad had a way of saying all of our names to make them sound like what we were to him. Like "Ivan y venian," his version of my name.

"Yes, Tony, what is it?" Mother said. She never called him Antonio or spoke to him in Spanish or pronounced his name in Spanish. Antonio was Tony to her, not Toño, like he was to Tía Vicki, or Toñito, like he was to Tía Lucia. He was just foursquare Tony like he'd come to Utah, where they met, on a covered wagon over the plains, instead of up through the desert like the bracero that he was.

Stepdad reached over and pinched Mother's arm.

"*Ya mero, eh, Margarona*," he said.

Almost there. The folds of her skin pulled back into a red spot. She pulled her arms back fast enough to shake the rest of her.

"What is it that you want, for god's sake, Tony?" she asked.

"*Nada, tu siempre te enojas*," he said in his *you're-such-a-bitch, I-can't-wait-to-get-a-beer* voice. *You always get mad.* His arm was like a stick at the top of the steering wheel, his wrist hovering over the bottom part of the wheel.

"Good God, don't get started." Mother's words came from the back of her throat like she was winching up a good spit.

In the seat behind Stepdad, I sat folded up small like the bags and sacks. With my back as a shield, I searched my head for thick and bumpy strands of hair amid the mix of strong and weak ones. One by one, I plucked them out, stretching them, then pulling them tight between my thumb and forefinger. I pulled the strand until I found the first split at the top of the strand and pulled the hair apart, millimeter by millimeter, all the way down.

Mother's slap came as a surprise.

"Goddamn it, you're going to go bald," she said.

I went flat and curled up again, hiding in the bags and sacks.

Mother waited to get her hair done at Olga's shop in Tijuana. It was cheaper and the hair spray kept longer. Olga's face was a deep, almost reddish brown, and you could tell she was one of Stepdad's Mazatlán cousins by the burned-even color of her skin and the way her bosom cut into her blouse. When she talked, her lips opened and closed like a child's handheld paper game, pink against brown. *Two, four, six, tell a fortune, make a wish.* Olga's hair was straight brown and streaked with gold. It curved around her round face against gold loop earrings, then opened up into a flip at the bottom. Her streaked gold hair and earrings matched the gold caps in the back of her mouth.

Olga was putting the finishing touches on a beehive flip when we got there. She lifted the strands of hair with the rat tail of a rat tail comb. Strands up, she teased it by pushing the hair against itself into a tuft. Rat tail lift, up, tease, tuft. Straight, untufted hair smoothed over the rat tail into a bubble. When it was high enough, Olga waved an institution-size can of Aqua Net hair spray over the bubble flip like a wand that magically changed the lady in her chair into a movie star like the ones on Olga's mirrors. Aqua Net made you a movie star for a week. A week of sleeping facedown on cushions with your hair under a pink net bubble protector.

In every one of Olga's six chair stations by the lean-back red sinks there were ladies wearing mesh wire-brush rollers that were held down with pink plastic sticks. The rows of rollers and pins under the metal-flake gold plastic dryers covered the ladies' heads like helmets.

At Olga's station, there were three mirrors with pictures with ladies in flips, bubbles, and Connie Francis beehives. Girls with girlie flips and velvet bows at the hairline between bangs and bubble. Pictures of ladies with soft brown Sophia Loren eyes, outlined in black, with thick, thick black eyelashes. Olga's eye shadow was gold-dust golden against reddish-brown skin that surrounded her open and closed pink-against-brown lips.

Olga kissed my mother on both cheeks. "Margarita," she said.

The centipede scar under my mother's arm rippled up under the folds of her skin when she lifted her arms to hug Olga and rippled down when she dropped her arms. Up and down, Mother's centipede scar never went anywhere.

Mother's hand on the bald spot on my head, her centipede arm on my shoulder, she pushed me forward to Olga. "*Aquí traigo la pelona*," she said. *Here's the bald one.*

Olga's pink-against-brown lips formed a line, then broke into a smile. Deep brown against the gold watch on her wrist, she put her hand on my splotchy arm. Her white coat opened like French doors over her red T-shirt. The red T-shirt outlined her hips. Olga's hips were wide in white bell-bottoms, the hemline of her red T-shirt stopping right above where her pants split for her legs, at the opening of her river.

Women in Mexico never seemed to care if their bosoms cut peaks into their blouses and their hips were round and moved with music only they heard. They didn't hunch over and fold their arms, or wear sacks for dresses and cover with long blouses the line where their rivers ran.

"*A ver.*" *Let's see*, she said. Her coat open, the inside smelled of her sweet sweat and perfume. She pushed my hair back behind my ears. Outside of her was nail polish, Aqua Net, and shampoo drying.

Olga's shop was a shrine to the patron saint of hopeless hair cases. She was Mother's last hope for me. A cure for the growing bald spot on my head, the mangled mess that was my uneven black wavy hair. In Olga's shop, your hair was what you were. Olga could read hair like people read palms.

"*No se que hacer con ella.*" *I don't know what to do with her*, Mother said. Her centipede arm rested in a fold with her other arm over her bosom. My legs locked and I couldn't move.

"*A ver, a ver.*" *Let's see, let's see*, Olga said. She pulled at the length of an uneven strand of my hair that had been left to hang when I ran off without permission to get a bad haircut. One hand on my bald spot and the other hand lifting up the chopped strand, Olga waved her magic arm over me. I was bald in one spot and too long in the other, that much was obvious. Mother refolded her centipede across her rounded bosom. Mother's bosom didn't poke out like Olga's. It rested there like a mound, a place for the centipede to rest, on top of her homemade cotton print shift.

Mother looked at Olga as if to say, *What do you think, Doc, can you even fix her up? Can you do something with her?*

Olga put her hands on my shoulders and pushed me back to see the rest of me. Olga looked back at Mother as if to say, *I hate to tell you this, Margaret, but the rest of this kid looks pretty crooked too, splotchy arms, dry gray skin on her elbow and knee*s.

Pink against brown, Olga's lips opened into a smile, and she pulled me close.

"*Un cariño, solo un cariño le falta esta niña,*" Olga said. *Simple kindness is all she needs.*

CHAPTER 18

LA MEDALLA

During the war, women slept in the rooms that circled the courtyard in front of La Doña's big yellow house. We sat in the afternoon shade of the patio near the rooms where the women once slept and where men came to visit them in the night. In rooms under roofs where happy plaster Buddhas now sat, their hands flat over their heads to hold up the sky and to dry in the hot Tijuana sun.

When Tío Miguel was a little boy, it was said that La Doña wore an apron with slots for hundreds, tens, and twenties. She never made change. If the going rate was fifteen bucks and you had a twenty, you could consider your extra five a gift to the orphan's relief fund. *Si no te gustaba,* if you didn't like it, La Doña pointed you to the door with the luger she parked in her triple-D, made-in-New-York-City longline brassiere. During the war, you came to La Doña's to spend money, not make change.

"*Está la tía y los primos,*" I could hear my cousin Chavela say. *Our aunt and cousins are here.*

In minutes, we were circled by blue-and-white Tigres de Tijuana baseball jerseys. My cousin's arm hung on my shoulder like it had a place there all its own.

Arm in arm, I felt her hips against mine. Her ruby-red pendant earrings matched her red fingernails. Here, it was okay for girls to hug each other and even to hold hands.

More cleats at the door, Tío Miguel walked down the steps. His baseball jersey stretched over his stomach, and his knees pulled up his striped blue-and-white jersey leggings. On his left shoulder, he carried my cousin Cruz, or Cruzita, Chavela's younger sister. On his right shoulder, he carried a trophy. Cruzita, a year younger than Chavela, jumped off his shoulder and ran over to us. Her purple rhinestone necklace hung over her top Tigres de Tijuana uniform button.

"*Prima, Prima,*" she said, circling her arms around me like a wreath.

"*Amá, ganámos,*" Tío Miguel said to La Doña. *We won.* He gave his mother the trophy, and La Doña set it on the table. There before us was a little golden statue of Cruzita, the team's star pitcher. She stood atop a pillar and pointed to the sky, like the Angel Moroni, but without the horn. Cruzita was dark-skinned like her dad. Her deep-brown amber hair curved behind her ears and cut into her face when she took her baseball cap off. Cruzita was her dad's girl as much as blond-haired Chavela was Tía Vicki's.

"Toño." Tío Miguel grabbed my stepfather's hand and pulled him in close. Tío took his baseball cap off with his other hand to complete his reach, the blue baseball cap pressed against my stepfather's back.

"*¿Cuando llegaron?*" Tío wanted to know when we'd gotten there. Drops of sweat poured down the side of his face. His arms completely around Stepdad, Tío lifted Stepdad off the ground and held him in the air in a bear hug. Stepdad touched the ground with a spring in his step and slapped Tío Miguel's back.

Tío Miguel reached over and kissed Tía Lucia on the cheek, his short-sleeve shirt tight against her white lace collar.

"*Mira, Toño trajo su equipo,*" he said. Stepdad nodded, yes, he'd brought his whole team.

Tío Miguel pulled out a handful of silver dollars and flipped one in the air for each of us to catch.

No one missed.

My brother Joe's eyes got wide like Little Orphan Annie. Ted quickly put his in his pocket and looked around to see who noticed where he put it. Izzy stared at his under the light in his flat, open hand. Sal caught his and dropped it. I don't remember what I did with mine.

"What do you say?" Stepdad prompted.

"Thanks, I mean, gracias, Tío Miguel," Joe said. We all nodded and said thank you.

Cousin Chavela took my hand and walked me over to Tía Lucia.

"*Tía,*" she said, "*ahora que está la prima, ¿podémos ir a comprar la tela?*" *Now that our cousin is here, can we go buy the embroidery linen?* Chavela's blond hair hung free from the braids she wore under her baseball cap.

"*Ándale, hija,*" Tía said. Tía pulled a folded bill out of her dress pocket. "*Vayanse las tres.*" *Go the three of you.*

Chavela took Cruzita's hand and mine. The three of us ran up to the big house through the kitchen and over the linoleum forest of dark flowers that was the living room floor and into the girls' bedroom. They took off their cleats and put on running shoes over their socks and flipped the baseball legging stirrups back over their calves. There was no time to change; we were on our way to buy linen and thread.

I ran down streets that had no name, streets that led to semi-paved roads and finally to sidewalks with high curbs. The *tortillería* steamed with the smell of hot cooked cornmeal and rendered pork rinds. At nearly every corner there were women with kids selling food from baskets. In the baskets that hung around the women's necks there were tamales, *pan dulce*, candy bars, and gum. Babies in *rebozos* on their backs. My cousins walked by the women like they weren't there.

"*No compres comida en la calle*," Chavela said. *Don't buy street food.* She rolled her hair up under her hat.

Cruzita flexed her pitching arm behind her and pulled me in close. "*La comida no es buena. Te enfermas*," she explained. *The food is no good. You'll get sick.*

We got to another corner, and I saw a woman with a baby wrapped tight around her back in a red *rebozo*. She sold yellow birds in wood-stick cages like the ones Great-Grandma Mercedes had in the restaurant when I was little. The woman balanced the birds on her head and carried a basket full of *caramelos* on her arm. She bent over, looking like a hunchback with the baby lump on her back under the weight of birds and candy.

My cousins held me close and moved me along, their hips and legs on each side of mine.

"*No tengo hambre; no quiero comprar nada*," I said. *I'm not hungry; I don't want to buy anything.*

I wanted the woman with the red *rebozo* to have lemonade with seeds, eggs with onions, tomatoes, and green peppers, hot tortillas, and a trophy with angel cousins on top.

At the end of the food carts in the cobblestone plaza market we walked and walked until there, in the shade of a giant church, was the red pushcart my cousins were looking for.

There were coconut candy squares with pink dyed topping, like the kind my great-grandma Mercedes sold in her Salt Lake City Mexican restaurant. There were little green jars of Four Roses hair pomade, the kind that Stepdad had worn the first time he asked Mother to dance. Mother said she didn't like him because he was from "the other side," but she danced with him anyway and remembered him because his hair smelled thick and kind of sweet. There were Chicklets that we were never allowed to bring home because they reminded Stepdad of Yankee soldiers who threw them to hungry kids on the streets of Tijuana when he was a boy. On the covers of pulp magazines stacked back-to-back next to the coconut candy and Four Roses pomade, there were pictures of mustached men chasing partially clothed women who fled under the title of *PELIGRO*.

On the pushcart poles, there were gold medal pendants of Our Holy Mother at one price and more Holy Mothers on another pole, at a different price. I reached for the inexpensive pendant to compare it to a more expensive one. I almost had the two pendants together in my hand when a woman reached from behind the pushcart and gripped my wrist with her gold bracelet hand.

"*¿Qué se le ofrece, niña?*" she said. *How can I help you, child?* The woman's voice broke my hold over the higher-priced Mother of God. I stared at the lower-priced Holy Mother and the baby Jesus in my hand.

"*¿Cuanto?*" I asked the woman. *How much?*

"No, *hija, no compres esa medalla,*" the woman said. *No, dear, don't buy that medal.* Going back to her lunch, the top of her apron smelling of grease and chili from the food stains, she wiped her mouth and hands with the skirt part of her apron, looked over at my cousins, and nodded her head toward me. I obviously wasn't from around here.

"No, *Prima, no compres esa medalla,*" my cousins said. The discount Mother of God was for heathens, tourists, and the unbaptized. And surely, I would want a Holy Mother that had been blessed in Rome.

"*Me parece lo mismo, y no le hace,*" I replied.

The Holy Mother looked the same to me, I said to my cousins, and I didn't care if she had been blessed in Rome, right here, or not at all. If she did need a blessing, I'd take her to the basilica myself.

My cousins laughed and gave the woman their own money to buy the pendant. If I insisted on walking around with an unblessed Holy Mother, they wanted to be sure to watch, so they paid the few centavos it cost to buy her. The woman reached her arms up to unhook the pendant. Her apron rose up over her bosom, and she pulled the pendant over the pole and handed the unholy Mother and baby Jesus to me.

The hot metal hit my chest. I pressed her close. An unblessed Virgen for an unblessed girl. I wanted to embed her in me like the relics buried in our sanctuary back home.

CHAPTER 19

DON PEDRO

We walked up the cobblestone path behind La Doña's yellow house and in front of the concrete room that had been assigned to us. I wanted to show my mother the thread and linen Tía Lucia bought for us.

Chavela stopped me. "*¿Alli van a dormir?*" she asked.

"Yes," I said. *That's where we are sleeping.*

My cousins pulled me over to a tree behind the house. We sat on a twisted stump. Chavela pulled her *tela* out of her bag and put it on her head.

"*Póngaselo como si estubieras en la misa,*" she said. *Put it on like you are in mass.*

"*¿Por qué?*" I asked. *Why?*

"*Hazlo, y ahora te digo,*" she whispered. *Do it, and I'll tell you.*

I wanted to know what she wanted to tell me and why she was whispering, so I did as she asked and put the tela on my head as if we were in mass, except at home I always lost my veil and had to make a run to the bathroom to get the little folded-up tissue squares out of the dispenser to put on my head with a bobby bin. Tela square or tissue squares, it really didn't matter, I never understood how toilet paper on your head made you holy anyway.

Cruzita put her tela on top of her baseball cap.

"*Ese cuarto era el cuarto de Don Pedro,*" Chavela said. *That room was Don Pedro's room.*

The concrete room was one of three rooms laid out side by side made of brick and mortar on the path up to the big house. There was a front door on each house and a window on the side of the end rooms and a window on the back of the middle room. Each room had a shower.

The room on the end belonged to Don Pedro. Don Pedro was their grandfather, and when Tía Vicki was a little girl and their aunt Ingracia wasn't born yet, Don Pedro ran off with another woman and squandered all their money. So, when he came back, years after Tía Victoria and her sister Ingracia were grown up with their own children, they really didn't know him.

An unraveled thread from the tela hovered over my eyebrow, and I reached for it. Why, I wanted to know, as I pulled at the thread, did telling me about Don Pedro running off mean that we had to sit under this tree with linen veils on our heads? I pulled; the linen thread got longer, and the corner of my tela frayed with little bits of corner-cut threads scattering down my dress over my breasts.

"*La razón, Prima,*" Chavela said, "*es un dicho de la tía, a veces lo sagrado viene escondidio.*"

What did Tía Lucia mean that sometimes the sacred is hidden? Hidden in what? And what did that have to do with sitting here under a tree with embroidery fabric veils on our heads?

Cruzita pushed back her tela veil. Her baseball cap cut shade across the back of her brown neck.

When he found Tía Vicki, she said, Don Pedro was sick and penniless with nowhere else to go. Tía Vicki asked La Doña if he could stay with them. They let him sleep in the room and brought him food because he was too ashamed to ask for any and sometimes would go for days without eating.

"*¿Por que lo recibío, mi tía?*" I asked. *Why did Tía Vicki take him in all those years after he left, after he spent all their money?*

"*Porque era su padre,*" Cruzita said. Cruzita and Chavela leaned over me, all big eyes and dimples. *Because he was her father.* Because it was her duty to take care of him, because you're always supposed to show respect for your father, no matter what he did, and anyway, the point was, Don Pedro hung himself.

I twisted my Limbo pendant, the unblessed discount Mother of God.

"*¿Donde?*" I asked. *Where?*

Tía Vicki found him in the shower. He'd been hanging there for a couple of days.

"*¿Qué paso?*" I asked. *What happened?*

She had him cut down and buried on the other side of the *cerro.* He lay there but nobody brought him flowers, lit candles, or said prayers for him. His body was there, but he'd been dead long before he got there, Tía Vicki told them, and it was the least she could do, be there when he left, the way he had been there when she was born.

"*¿Podémos ir a verlo?*" I asked. I wanted to see where Don Pedro was buried.

"*¿Por qué?*" they said. *Why?*

I twisted my pendant again. At least Don Pedro came back, I told them, so Tía Vicki would know where he was buried.

Cruzita's brown eyes widened, and Chavela rubbed the bumps off her arm.

"*Véngase,*" Chavela said, pulling my arm. *Come on.* My cousins and I held our tela veils down so they wouldn't fly off, and we walked to the other side of the cerro to the lonely mound of rocks that marked Don Pedro's last place in the earth.

Chavela and Cruzita picked up a rock and placed it on the flattened pile. There were already enough rocks to hold Don Pedro in place for a long, long time, but they just wanted to be sure.

We took the long dirt path back over the cerro. I took my tela veil off and pushed it into one of the square-edged pockets on the front of my dress. I put the embroidery thread in the other. I told my cousins I'd be right back. I was just going to show the thread and linen to my mother.

I pulled the door to Don Pedro's room open. Mother sat on the end of the bed. The back of her rose-print sundress was unzipped, and she reached back to snap her bra. My stepfather was standing. He buttoned the top of his pants. The silver belt buckle on his long black leather belt hung in front of him. He tucked in his white shirt. The blankets on the wide brown painted metal bed were twisted up in the middle like a hurricane. Mother turned. Her lipstick was pushed to one side of her lips, and her hair was dented.

"What are you doing here?" She pulled at her zipper, and I felt my words catch in the silver teeth.

"Did I call you?" she said. She pulled again at her zipper, and my tongue flattened.

"No, Mom, I just . . ." I said. I felt the nipples push against my training bra. My armpits dampened. Mother stood up and turned to face me. Her hands were behind her back. She held her dress down with one hand and pulled the metal zipper up to close her dress with the other.

"Well, get the hell out of here. And from now on, knock before you come in here. Do you understand me?" she said. Her voice hit the walls of the room like the bullhorn voice we'd heard from a flatbed politician on Election Day, everywhere but nowhere.

I stepped back into the doorway and felt the midday heat against my sleeveless shoulders.

I twisted the tela between my fingers and walked backward out of the room onto the steps. My cousins had been waiting outside, waiting to share in the joy of my new needlework project. This time, like other times, the reactions they got from their parents did not match what I got from mine.

Chavela's face flashed pink then red across her cheeks, and Cruzita's lip quivered. Their arms around me, we walked over to their house and down the flowered linoleum hall to their bedroom. They sat me on top of one of the beds with all the blankets and then climbed up to sit on each side of me. I pulled at my hair with one hand and held the tela in the other.

Chavela grabbed my hand with her golden-haired arm and held it. "*Te vas a volver pelona*," she said. *You are going to go bald.*

I didn't care if I was going bald.

They sat next to me, their striped leggings against my dusty white cotton skirt.

"*Prima, no te procupes. Aquí estas con nosotras,*" they said. *Cousin, don't worry, you are here with us now.* On the bed with them, I didn't feel scared or even worried about what Mother might still have to say to me. They smoothed my choppy hair and dabbed my eyes with the corners of their telas.

The room was cursed, they said, and hadn't been blessed since Don Pedro hung himself in it. Tío Miguel said it didn't need blessing because in the eyes of God, Don Pedro had lost his soul and was already dead when he got there. La Doña said that it should be blessed anyway, because if it wasn't blessed it would continue to attract bodies with no spirits and people with no souls. Why else had Don Pedro come from all over Mexico and the United States to find his daughter after so many years to plague her with his death, if not for that room in need of blessing?

I pulled my cousins' heads toward me, one hand on Cruzita's curved auburn silk and the other on Chavela's blond braid.

I had my own experience with the cursed room. In the middle of it there was a large brown bed with curved metal at the top of the bed and at the bottom. The metal bed base served as a kind of partition. Our beds were all around it like little matchboxes. Nine of us were supposed to slide into our matchboxes of sleep and not notice anything in the room except the cold-water shower at the end of the room.

It was the sand that I could never wash off that I remember most about that shower. The shower that Don Pedro hung himself in. Where Tía Victoria found him when he didn't come out for his food.

In the courtyard one day, one of the kids who chased the dead chicken with us said that a lady was going to have sex with a donkey at a nightclub. That sounded so crazy, like the stories in the *Tales from the Crypt* graphic novels my brothers read. Stories so fantastical, weird, and creepy, you half believed what they said and only dared to read them.

One night, Mother and Stepdad got all dressed up to go out with Tío Miguel and Tía Victoria. Mother's hair was shellacked in place like a helmet. Stepdad could dress as Tijuanero as he wanted, with flamboyant mismatched clothes, two-tone wing tips, and white socks. He was in Tijuana, after all.

We were in our matchboxes in the still dark of early morning when the station wagon lights shone through the windows and then went off. It was a while before my parents walked in. Then I heard Mother whisper, "Stop, the kids are asleep. Just go to bed, Tony. The kids are asleep. Stop it."

Mother went to the shower room to change her clothes. Stepdad grabbed the end of the brown metal bed and pulled himself onto the mattress, taking off his shirt, pants, and shoes.

I scooted as far as I could into my matchbox, pulling the blankets over me. After what felt like the longest time, Mother came out of the shower room in her nightgown. She checked to see if Stepdad was asleep and walked around the bed to her side. As soon as she lay down, he grabbed for her.

"No, Tony. No, the kids . . ."

He pulled himself on top of her.

"No, stop," she said.

But he didn't, pushing himself on her, harder and harder until he was done and rolled off to sleep and started to snore. Mother got up and went back to the shower room.

The next morning, I got up early before the rooster crowed to get the first shower to wash off the sand. I could feel it in my hair, under my arms, on my back, in my toes, sand everywhere that wouldn't come off. The cold water hit hard, harder than I could stand it sometimes, but no matter how long I could make myself stand there, I couldn't get the sand off. I pulled the towel down, and it had sand in it too.

When I walked out of the shower, Stepdad and the boys had gone outside to pee. Mother was taking the blankets off the brown metal bed. I looked over the brown metal bed base and saw a large bloodstain. I looked up at Mother, and before I could meet her gaze, she reached over the brown metal bed and slapped me so hard my wet, stringy hair whipped my face over the sting of the slap. I folded myself into the sandy towel and dragged myself to my matchbox. Naked, cold, and full of sand I couldn't wash off.

Chavela jumped off the bed and walked over to the pile of clothes on the tables and pulled out a plastic bag. Inside the bag there was another bag, a brown sack. In that bag there was a folded ruffled lavender tulle tie-back dress, my Easter dress from last year.

"*Mira, Prima, tu vestido,*" Cruzita said. Chavela held the dress up to me see if it fit.

I touched the white silk flower on the sash and the lace-edged ruffles that ran up each side of the bodice. The dress had been kept lying in state, waiting for me, since last year.

Cruzita jumped off her bed. She and Chavela pulled at me with one brown arm and one white arm. I threw my dress over my shoulder and jumped down too. They pulled me into their mother's room where a large wooden wardrobe opened to a full-length oval mirror. They unzipped my crooked three-step placket, Simplicity-pattern zipper and pulled it down over buckles and bumps so it wouldn't catch against my slip. I stood in front of the mirror in my full slip with the little pink roses on the front. The roses matched the Tuesday panties I wore on Saturday, because I could never keep the days straight. My strap ends flipped out, and I had to fold them back around the metal catch on the strap. Cruzita raised my arms, and Chavela put the dress over my head. The ruffles lay against my face, and my cousins struggled to shimmy the dress down over my shoulders. The ruffles in my face smelled like my cousins. The dress down, my cousins pulled the fabric in the back together to close the zipper. The fit was tight around the bodice. I reached over to look, and the hem was higher than I remembered.

My cousins turned me to face the mirror.

"*Mira, Prima, todavia te queda tu vestido.*" *Look, cousin, your dress still fits you.* My cousins were so excited about my dress still kind of fitting me, they clapped and did a pogo dance. There in front of the mirror with my Tigres de Tijuana cousins on each side of me, I stood to look at myself in my too-tight-at-the-top Judy Garland Dress.

The kitchen door slammed, and we could hear Mother and Tía Vicki in the kitchen, where they liked to sneak cigarettes when Stepdad and Tío Miguel were gone.

My cousins pushed me through the door to the kitchen where Mother and Tía Vicki were.

"*Mira, Tía, mira, Mama, todavia le queda el vestido a mi prima.*" They were so excited that my dress still fit me, they wanted Mother and Tía to see. Mother put her cigarette out and rubbed the centipede scar under her arm.

"Go take that dress off," she told me. "It doesn't fit you anymore."

CHAPTER 20

THE ROAD RUNNER

"*Sientate, hija,*" Tía Lucia said. She pressed Irma's head against her shoulder for a rest and lifted Irma's bare legs over her lap. Tía called me over to see Irma's patterns. There were yellow roses outlined in gold. There were spiders all around the edges and a lonely, lonely tree. There were borders at the top and the bottom.

Tía wanted me to see how moving one space in either direction of the bow pattern changed the pattern's dimensions.

"*Así es la vida, hijas. Un cambio que parece inconsequente puede desorientar todo,*" she said. *That is how life is, daughters. A seeming inconsequential change can disorient everything.*

I looked at my tela bows and tried to see if making one small change in either direction could do anything more than make the bows bigger or smaller. *What did she mean life is like that, that what appears to be an inconsequential change can disorient everything?* I looked over to see what I might see in her tela but could only see what I saw in mine.

"*Ademáss, te puede mandar por otro camino entero,*" she said. *It could send you down a whole other path.*

I stared at my tela. It was hard to see how anything in it had the power to send me anywhere but right here in the morning shade with Tía Lucia and Silent Irma. Tía's woven gray-and-white braid hung around her shoulder. Her thin brown arms held Irma and me, Irma at her side in the chair and me standing next to Tía on the other side of the chair. In the quiet of Irma's sewing and Tía Lucia's mysteries in the tela, there was no place else to go. With Tía's arm around my waist, I knew that whatever I was going to find in the tela would make sense when it needed to.

Up the road, Tío Miguel's truck curved up the cobblestone path in front of where we were sitting. Stepdad and Tío Miguel rode in the cab. There were two rifles in the rack in the back of the window of the truck. My brother Joe, cousin Fidel, and Fidel's dog Coco rode in the truck bay.

Cousin Fidel's white skin was the same shade as his mother's, his hair straight and black like Tío Miguel's. His dog Coco, like Fidel, was white all over except around his eyes. Cousin Fidel sat in what looked like his usual spot under the gun rack next to the toolbox. My brother sat in the corner and held on to the sides of the truck.

Something lifeless and gray lay on top of the toolbox and hit the bumps as the truck moved up the path.

Tío Miguel drove around the back of the yellow house where the cobblestone road ended and where the dirt road started, by where the pigs and chickens were, and up to the courtyard where the ceramics workers were mixing, pouring, and casting piggy bank toros.

In the courtyard, a little boy with no shoes carried two buckets of water on a pole over his shoulders. Two other boys carried bags of plaster. There were rubber molds of all the animals we had seen at the border: frogs, burros, pigs, and long feline cats with gold whiskers. The courtyard was wet with water and stained with plaster. Tío Miguel parked the truck in the middle of the courtyard and jumped out. Stepdad slammed the truck door shut, closed his hand around a brown sack, and pushed it into his pocket. The kids with water and plaster got out of his way. Some of the ceramics workers nodded and tipped their hat to Tío, but most just moved on, not looking up at him at all.

My brother Joe jumped out of the truck and ran to the doorway of the courtyard by where I was sitting with Tía and Silent Irma.

"Tío Miguel shot a rabbit," he said to me in a low voice so I would be the first to know.

My brother's eyes, always so full, were bigger now. When he wasn't talking about dead rabbits, his pupils fell to the bottom of his big white eyes like cherries in the bottom of a bowl.

My brother stood in the doorway and raised his head and his voice like the time he sang the solo in "Kyrie, Lord Have Mercy," at High Mass on Easter Sunday. He'd stood in the choir loft in a white dress over a white cassock, his nimble, lonely voice falling over all of us, still not believing it was him.

"Tío Miguel caught a rabbit, and they're gonna kill a chicken for us to eat," he said.

He raised his arm and pointed to the pole in the middle of the courtyard where Tío Miguel had hung the rabbit. The rabbit's ears had been tied together by twine and the rabbit hung there, its eyes open and belly forward. My brother ran back to the knot of kids that stood around the pole. The kids had sticks in their hands and beat them against the pole and on the ground under the dead rabbit. I left my tela bows behind with Tía to see what was happening.

In the last room of the row of rooms that circled the court-yard, Doña Evelina held an axe up to a stone wheel. She pushed the pedal of the stone wheel with her foot. Her skirt moved up and down, even with a back-and-forth motion. The axe blade cut sparks around the stone. She leaned forward and backward, the axe against the turning wheel, again and again.

Kids, dogs, and smiling ceramic Buddhas were everywhere.

Tía Vicki walked out into the court from the other side of the house by where the chickens and pigs were and went around to Tío Miguel's truck. She held a white feathered chicken under her arm and walked over to Tío Miguel and Stepdad.

"¿Quien lo sacó?" she asked.

Stepdad nodded his head to Tío. "Un tiro, solo un tiro," he said. Stepdad shrugged, drew his hands up to Tio Miguel, and pulled back like he had fired a rifle. Tío Miguel had taken the rabbit out with one shot.

"No hubo chansa," Stepdad said. "Ni pa mi, ni el conejito." No chance, he said, not for him or the rabbit.

Tía Vicki laughed.

"Porteño" Tío Miguel said. He lifted his hand to smooth back his hair.

Stepdad grew up in the port city of Mazatlán. He was better at fish than rabbits.

Tío Miguel took his knife from the leather side pocket that hung at the waist of his jeans and walked it over to the wheel. He ran it against the sharpening stone a few times. When the flint sparks stopped flying, he walked over to the rabbit that hung with its ears tied from the pole.

He made one slit across the top of the rabbit's chest, a line down the middle of his stomach to make a T, and then a slit below the bulge of the bowl that had gathered at the bottom. He cut the rabbit open like a travel-size box of Rice Krispies. When Tío Miguel cut the line into the bottom of the rabbit's belly, he pulled back on the rabbit's tail and a braid of gray steamy guts spilled out onto the plaster-stained concrete of the courtyard.

The chicken's white breast heaved in and out next to Tía Vicki's white cotton blouse. Tía Vicki held the chicken's yellow beak shut with her hand. The flattened chicken's wings lay still under her arm. The only thing that moved on the chicken were its feet. Its eyes got wider and wider the closer Tía got to Doña Evelina.

The ceramics workers nodded to Doña Evelina and Tía Vicki and moved white unpainted newly cast piggy bank animals to the roof for drying. They moved dried cats and parrots off the roof to the painting table in the sun. The tall, narrow felines were spray-painted all black and then hand-brushed with gold to outline their paws and to scroll on eyes and whiskers. The parrots hung on their plaster poles and were spray-painted green and hand-painted to make red, blue, and yellow feathers.

Above the painted cats and parrots, the long neck of the rabbit hung on a big hook on the pole next to the sharpening wheel where Doña Evelina cut the last sparks on the axe. There was a bullet hole in the side of the rabbit's head.

"You have to aim for the head so you don't mess up the meat," Joe said. His eyes got big again like the movie of the rabbit's shooting played before him.

Doña Evelina walked the axe over to the wooden stump under the pole. Behind the pole where the rabbit hung, white plaster full-belly Buddhas sat in row after row on the roof. The white Buddha smiled, a coin slot on its head.

Tía Vicki handed Doña Evelina the chicken. Doña Evelina took the chicken and smoothed the feathers on its head and neck.

"*Pollito, Pollito*," she said.

The chicken legs stopped kicking, and its wings slowed down. Just when it looked like the chicken was ready to jump off her aproned hip and fly back to its coop, Doña Evelina grabbed its head with one hand. She bent over, her skirt lowering a curtain over her bare legs, which stood in untied work boots. She bent over farther with the chicken head in her hand and turned her wide basket hips. The back curtain of her skirt rose up behind her to drop a white cotton slip over the top of her white calves.

She grabbed the chicken's neck like it was the handle on a noisemaker and swung the chicken's body around and around like a whip. When the chicken's body was in motion in a white circle, she pulled her wrist back until the chicken's neck snapped.

The chicken's breast caved in, and its eyes rolled back. The chicken's body and head lay in Doña Evelina's arms in two sections connected by the bent neck, one feathery body and a smaller slow-breathing head. Doña Evelina walked the chicken to the wooden stump. The chicken's wings flapped a little, and its feet opened and closed. She held the head and the body down.

Doña Evelina picked up the axe and dropped it on the chicken's neck, once, then twice. She picked up the chicken's head and threw it to the dogs. Coco caught the chicken's head in his mouth in midair; he opened his jaw to get a better grip and held the chicken's head between his teeth. Chicken eyes and dog's teeth. Coco did a home run slow trot around the courtyard. No other dogs even tried.

Doña Evelina took the chicken body off the stump and set the chicken on its feet. The headless chicken walked around and around, poking out what was left of its neck. The chicken was still trying to be a chicken. Its head was gone, but the chicken's body didn't know that.

The kids with sticks followed the chicken on her *borracha* walk.

"*Pollo muerto, pollo muerto,*" they shouted. *Dead chicken, dead chicken.*

The headless chicken's body walked in a big circle in the middle of the courtyard over the plaster stains and water puddles, under the Buddhas and donkeys until it fell over by the ceramic Holy Mothers. The ceramic Holy Mothers stood around the chicken with open arms as if to welcome her home.

Doña Evelina picked the chicken up, its feet still kicking, and took it back to the wooden stump. She picked the axe up again and dropped it on the chicken's feet. The kids in the courtyard reached up for the feet. Doña Evelina threw one to my brother Joe. The red wrinkled chicken foot fell on him, and when he tried to catch it, he dropped it. Cousin Fidel picked it up for him and held it in his closed hand. Doña Evelina threw the other foot to the courtyard kids, who caught it and ran under the house with it.

Fidel opened his hand, and the wrinkled chicken foot lay flat. He pulled a tendon that stuck out of the stem of the chicken's foot, making the chicken's foot open and close like the gripper at the penny arcade. Fidel pulled and closed the chicken foot and walked it over Joe's head. Joe slapped it out of his hand, picked it up by a toe, and almost knocked over an armload of painted parrots to chase Ted with it.

Tía Vicki picked up the headless and footless chicken and walked it over to a bench on the shady side of the house, where she put the chicken in a bucket of boiling water. When the shade shifted, she pulled the chicken out and put it in her lap over her apron, between her bare legs. She pulled and pulled until all the chicken's feathers came off.

That night at the picnic table in La Doña's kitchen, we sat down for our supper. We looked at the chicken mole on our plates and the bowl of hot rabbit stew my uncle, aunt, and cousins served themselves. Joe scanned his saucer eyes up at Stepdad, then back to his plate. Stepdad rolled up his tortilla and poured chili on his bowl of the stew. Joe looked at me, and we looked at Ted.

Ted's straight black hair always pointed into a beak in his hairline.

"Dad," Ted said.

Ted was the only one of us with a chance to say anything to Stepdad because he never got in trouble like we did, because he was dark-skinned like Stepdad and because Stepdad named him after Stepdad's favorite Mexican, Cantinflas, Mario Moreno, next to José Mojica and Lola Beltrán, of course.

"Dad, do we have to eat the Road Runner?" Ted asked.

Stepdad dipped his tortilla into the rabbit stew like he didn't hear Ted. I pushed the chicken to one side of my plate and moved the beans and rice around to make it look like I was eating something. Joe put a piece of chicken in the back of his throat and washed it back with water. I looked at him. His eyes got bigger than usual, like they did when got ready to cry.

Stepdad lifted a spoon of stew to his mouth.

"Dad, are you going to make us eat Bugs Bunny?" Ted asked. Ted put his spoon down and watched Stepdad's mouth.

Stepdad opened his mouth around the spoon of stew, then closed it and dropped his spoon into his bowl. Stepdad stared at all of us.

"You don' wanna eat?" he said.

We looked down at our plates. A silver dollar–sized tear was ready to break out of Joe's eye.

Tío Miguel took a tortilla in his hand and rolled it tight with a single two-hand motion. He pinched two ears at the end of the tortilla and gave it to Joe. Joe dipped the butt of his rabbit tortilla into his beans, not touching the chicken mole, and bit the tail of his tortilla off. I liked the way that tortillas mashed back up into dough even after they were cooked.

"I'm saving the ears," he whispered to Ted.

Ted poked his chicken with a fork. Joe dipped another section of his tortilla into the beans.

Stepdad leaned both arms against the picnic table.

"Get the hell out of here!" he said.

We put our spoons down, got up from the table, and walked quickly through the linoleum forest out of the kitchen.

CHAPTER 21

SANDY

Only the World Series kept Stepdad on the couch in front of the Zenith in the middle of the afternoon on a Tuesday or Wednesday, away from the railroad where his gang repaired track mostly in LA but sometimes as far out as Barstow. We knew it was fall when we got home from school and there he'd be on Mother's aqua metal-flake sectional with a big bag of peanuts and a beer.

"Hon ron!"

"Heckere meckere, you guys home already?" he'd say to us when we walked in short of breath and covered in a layer of silt from the LA smog.

On paid holidays and weekends, Stepdad picked up extra work pumping gas at the Union 76 gas station downtown across the street from the Shrine Auditorium. During the World Series he brought home promotional drinking cups with baseball players' faces on them encased behind see-through plastic. At dinner, we stared at the faces of the orange ball Union 76 season favorites. Carl Yastrzemski was popular at our table.

He didn't leak. The Alou brothers, Felipe, Marty, and Jesús, all leaked. Even Don Drysdale and Maury Wills leaked.

Sandy Koufax didn't leak, but we didn't use him. One morning, the *Los Angeles Herald Examiner* had a cover shot of Sandy with his arm in a bucket of ice. Stepdad lifted the newspaper up close to his face, close enough to hide his mustache.

"Sandy's losing his arm," Stepdad announced.

Stepdad rolled front-page Sandy up and held him close under his lunch pail under his arm. He walked down the red steps of our bungalow to his car like he was going to go take care of it first thing that morning on his way to work.

"We need him to play every game, and he doesn't play on Jewish holidays," Stepdad said.

He swung the gate closed behind him. Before he got into his car, he pulled newspaper Sandy from under his arm and pointed him at us.

"This is a man of principle who suffers for his sport," Stepdad said.

He got in his car and put his lunch pail on the passenger seat. He slid folded-up Sandy next to his lunch pail and drove off.

That night at dinner, we had *fideos* in tomato sauce laced with slivers of fried bologna with rice and beans on the side. The player cups were around the kitchen table like on a baseball diamond. We hunched over our plates with fresh, hot tortillas in hand.

Stepdad walked in from work, put his lunch pail on his chair at the head of the table, and went to the back sink to scrub the tar off his hands with the dirty bubble Lava soap that lived there.

Before he sat down to eat that day, he reached over and took Sandy's orange ball Union 76 baseball cup off the kitchen table, emptied out the grape Kool-Aid that left a gray stain inside it, and placed Sandy on the cupboard shelf above the kitchen table. All that season we folded, tore, and dipped our tortillas under Stepdad's shrine to Sandy Koufax.

"*Pinches Dodgers pendejos*," Stepdad said.

The lousy, stupid Dodgers, Stepdad hated them. They had no Latino players, not like the San Francisco Giants who had Juan Marichal. He railed against the Dodgers' every slight to the dignity of the Mexican people and to the whole of the Americas.

"Good God, it's only baseball for Chrissake," Mother said. "And will you watch your language in front of the kids?"

Mother shook the salt-and-pepper corduroys that everybody called khakis. She had me pull them off the clothesline so she could lay them flat, folding them seam to seam to make creases in the middle of the pant leg. Mother laid the pants under the couch cushions on the aqua sectional so we could press the pants while we sat on them in front of the Zenith.

"*Ni modo*," Stepdad said. *No choice.* "I gotta take 'em, Margaret," he said. He said Mother's name stretching out the syllables to make "Mar-gar-et" stretch out to sound like "cigarette." "It's a big game *si Drysdale quiebra su recor*," he said. Drysdale could break a record.

"Not on a school night," Mother said.

Mother pushed the cushions back into place, careful not to mess up the lined-up pant creases.

"We leave de stadium as soon de game over," Stepdad said.

Mother's hands pressed against the faded print pockets of her homemade shift dress, the ones she made from the cheap Woolworth fabric, five at a time.

"I don't care about Drysdale's record, what about the money?" Mother asked.

One by one, Stepdad pushed us out the door, down the red steps into the station wagon.

"*No me gusta darles a los pendejos mi dinero*," he said.

He hated giving the stupid Dodgers his money, but this was a game not to be missed. There was no time to change out of our uniforms before we got there and headed to the cheap seats.

My big black coat with the fake fur collar was my only

protection against the rain. It covered my starched white blouse and pleated red plaid uniform and hung over my white Shinola shoe-shined tennis shoes like a tent. I lifted my shoes, stiff with shine, into the wagon and prayed it wouldn't rain hard.

We made it to the stadium and parked far enough away to walk there so the car wouldn't heat up and die in the slow crawl into and out of the stadium. We made it there. Getting back was for later.

The rain started slowly when we got out of the car, and I pulled my coat around my shoes to keep the rain off, so my shoes wouldn't dissolve into Shinola silhouettes in the sidewalk where I walked. Oxfords would have held up against the rain, but there weren't any the price of the no-label canvas tennies, not even at Mother's favorite secondhand shop.

The stadium lights lit up like rows of Sylvania Blue Dot Flashcubes. The stadium floor was green, ballpark green, and the diamond looked like a diamond, its edge cut at the corners. People filed in from everywhere.

The peanut man wore a tray of hot peanuts around his neck. The roasted peanuts bunched up side to side like wooden soldiers in red striped uniforms. Hot oil seeped through the red bags. Hot and oil and salt hit me before I heard the peanut man.

"Peanuts, peanuts. Get your hot roasted peanuts!"

We climbed higher and higher to get to the seats on our tickets. The higher we got, the smaller the players on the field, until they were almost the size of my brothers' toy army men. I pulled my fake fur collar around my face and looked over the heads and hats of the people in front of us. When we got to our seats, Stepdad stood in front of us and leaned his face into us, his back to the baseball diamond and the crowd below. He pulled his ticket out of his pocket.

"You guys hold on to your tickets no matter what happens. Put it somewhere safe. If you get lost, look on your ticket and come back here. You understand? Here."

Stepdad pointed to our seats.

"The number to your seat is right there on your ticket," he explained.

We pulled our tickets out.

"W-15," Stepdad said. "My ticket says W-15. What does your ticket say, Ivan y venian?"

"My ticket says W-16," I replied.

"Good, they are in order," Stepdad said. "W-15, 16, 17. Got it?" He then turned toward the diamond and pointed his arms over the people in the rows and rows below us.

"Now," he said, "look out there and see where the empty seats are. Those are our seats."

Little pockets of seats, singles, doubles, and triples, appeared. Stepdad pointed to the section in front of us marked off by pillars at each end and the break of stairs on each side of the bleachers.

"Stay in this section," he said. "If you get lost, look on your ticket and come back here. Okay? Okay, let's go."

Ted put his ticket in my pocket. I could feel our tickets leave my hand and fall to the bottom of my long black coat pocket. I reached in to make sure that the tickets were there. The pocket was longer than my arm, and I stretched all the way down to find the tickets. The tickets hung there in the dark of my pocket like feathers.

Ted, Joe, and I ran past the peanut man, past the soda man, and past the hot dog man. Past all the people with binoculars around their necks, their blankets, seat pads, and radios. The wood-slat stadium benches were red, then blue, then green.

When we were done running, I looked over to find Stepdad not far away, a row down, five seats over. Izzy was on his lap. Izzy's red-and-black plaid jacket arm lay against the back of Stepdad's blue work coat. Ted and I took a pair of seats on the red benches. Joe was on the green bench behind us. I pointed to Stepdad so Ted and Joe could see him.

People around us started to stand.

Ted's hand was cold. Joe was behind us.

A woman with a big button at the top of her coat had her purse on the seat next to us. She reached over to Joe. "Would you like to sit next to your sister, son?"

Joe nodded.

"The seat next to me is empty," the woman said. "Why don't you sit here?"

She took her purse off the seat, and Joe jumped over the green bench to sit next to us on the red bench.

The music got louder, and all the people were standing. I looked to see where Stepdad was. At first, I couldn't see him with all the people standing around us. I let go of Ted's hand and reached into my pocket. I pushed deep to find the tickets with the numbers on them and stood up on my tiptoes, cracking the hardened shine of my white tennies. I held the tickets between my fingers and stepped higher to see over the people in front of me.

The stadium organ music started, and a woman came out on to the field in a glittering red dress and shoes that looked like ruby slippers. The woman on the field pulled the mic off the stand and stepped up to the pitcher's mound.

"*O say can you see . . .*"

Now everybody between and around us was standing.

"*By the dawn's early light . . .*"

I stood on the bench to see and found Stepdad. He was sitting down.

"*The bombs bursting in air . . .*"

Stepdad didn't move.

"*Gave proof through the night . . .*"

Izzy was on Stepdad's lap. Izzy in red and black waved back to us.

"*That our flag was still there . . .*"

Joe sat down.

"*For the land of the free . . .*"

I pulled away from Ted and put my hand over my heart. My heart buried under my black coat, under my red plaid surplice, under my starched white blouse, under my slip, under my skin.

A guy behind Stepdad and in front of us spat peanut shells down the front of his own coat and onto Stepdad's blue collar. "Hey, buddy, this is America, yer supposed to stand up for the flag," he said to Stepdad.

Stepdad turned and slapped the peanut shells off his blue jacket. "It's not my flag," he replied.

"Hey, too bad," the peanut spitter said.

The woman next to Joe pulled her coat tight around her neck. "Just leave it alone, will ya? We're here to enjoy the game," she said.

"*The land of the free . . .*"

"Can't you see they're just a bunch of wetbacks?" she said.

"*And the home of the brave . . .*"

Stepdad didn't move. We didn't move.

At eleven, I didn't make the connection, but over time I came to understand that my stepdad's refusal to stand for the flag was his stand, in this case, his sit-in, against the bigoted country we lived it. He took a stand like Sandy did, not against anybody but for himself and for us. I don't know if his action was inspired by Sandy, because we never discussed it, but I have no doubt that Sandy's demonstration of self-respect had an impact on my stepdad.

I didn't know that my eleven-year-old fixation on Sandy was actually a crush, since it was forbidden to think in those terms. Regardless, when I became a union rep, that crush grew into full-on fan fanaticism when I read Marvin Miller's book *A Whole Different Ball Game*, about the unionization of Major League Baseball.

Miller was the players' rep, a trained economist who was instrumental in unionizing the league. He recounts the early days of organizing when Sandy and Don Drysdale led one of the nascent baseball union's first job actions, the holdout.

In 1965, Sandy was being paid $70,000 a season, far less than the $130,000 being paid to Willie Mays in San Francisco. In addition to that, Sandy and Don got tired of being pitted against each other in their bargaining with the owners, so they joined together to hold out until they got what they wanted. It was Don's wife, Ginger Drysdale, who came up with the idea. Don and Sandy eventually got a better deal, and Miller credits this action as significant to the league's organizing: "The Koufax-Drysdale holdout during spring training had been an important rallying point for the players."

Miller goes on to quote a player talking about how the baseball owners overplayed them and comments that had Sandy been able to play in an "era of five-man rotations and relief specialists, it's entirely possible he could have played more seasons." And no doubt made more money, as Miller also notes.

But the event that turned Sandy's Union 76 baseball cup into a de facto shrine in our kitchen was the 1965 World Series, when Sandy decided not to play the first game of the series because it fell on Yom Kippur, the Jewish Day of Atonement.

By that time, we lived in Boyle Heights, a neighborhood that had once been a Jewish neighborhood, and the main street, now Avenida Cesar Chavez, was, as I remembered it as a kid, called Brooklyn Avenue. We'd moved "up" out of South Central LA to the Eastside, and the Jews had moved west to Fairfax and Santa Monica.

We'd walk by the boarded-up and gated Breed Street Shul right off of Brooklyn Avenue and wonder what kind of building it was and why nobody used it or took care of it. To borrow a phrase, as Mexican Catholic working-class kids "we didn't know from Yom Kippur," but we knew enough about Stepdad's respect for Sandy that it meant something for Sandy not to play on that day.

I can still see my stepdad holding up that copy of the *Herald Examiner* with Sandy's picture on it.

Three years later, John Carlos would hold up his fist at the '68 Olympics, and in 2018 Colin Kaepernick was locked out of the NFL for taking a knee to protest police racial violence.

Fifty-three years after the 1965 World Series, the late Marvin Miller, union organizer, economist, baseball union players' rep, and also Jewish, has time and time again been turned down for admission into the Baseball Hall of Fame. In organizing the league, Miller, along with leaders of the union, like Sandy and Don and East Bay's own Curt Flood (who led the fight against the reserve clause), did more for the players than any owner ever did. It was time that his contribution got recognized too, that he finally got admitted to the Baseball Hall of Fame.

Over fifty years later, as I reflect on what I learned from my stepdad and his love for baseball and all that went with it, I have to say that my knowledge of the game is limited to that era, to that narrow strip of time, so I apologize to all baseball fact fanatics for any errors.

I also gained some insight into my attraction to Jewish men, as Sandy was my first crush, a man of principle who suffered for his sport. When I became a union rep, I fell in love with him all over again, because he was a player's player, a union man, and a mensch. I did eventually marry a Jewish man and subsequently learned that I, too, was Jewish, if only in part. I was a descendant of the hidden Jews forced to change their names and hide their religion to escape the Inquisition. I descend from Indigenous people of Mexico who also had to hide to survive. They hid their own icons under the altars they were forced by the Spaniards to build and to worship in. Like the Jews, they had to either hide or die. During the first Sedar I attended as an adult, I could not stop crying. I was overwhelmed. The narrative alone was compelling: Having to spend forty years in the desert to unlearn your slavery. These friends took me to High Holiday services where I felt at home in some odd way, not yet knowing my DNA heritage.

What Sandy did when he refused to play that day was to come out of hiding in a very public way. When he did, part of me did too.

POSTSCRIPT: Marvin Miller was inducted into the Baseball Hall of Fame in 2020.

CHAPTER 22

NEVER RUN AFTER A BUS

The cab ride to Grandma Mary's from the bus station was notable for the crick in my neck as I stretched it out the window to take in a city so compact that everything was built up to the sky. I'd never seen such ornate, beautiful buildings. In contrast to horizontal LA, Grandma's city was vertical in a way just as vast. The chipped paint and the too-red lips on some of the fading Victorians were like her, a painted lady past her prime.

I'd made it. I'd finally escaped my mother's house. Grandma waited for me behind the lobby door and walked out to the street as I got out of the cab in front of her building. She paid the driver as I took my bag from the back seat.

"Ivana," she said, leaning in to greet me. Her lips were wide, flat, shiny, and smooth against my cheek. "Welcome to Frisco, but don't call it Frisco. The locals don't like it when you say Frisco," she added.

I pulled my bags into the lobby. She insisted we stop by the corner market right next to her building.

The heavy wooden door to her building was solid, old, and familiar; it was substantial in a way no flimsy LA door was. We took the granite steps down to the street and up the curved marble corner steps to the market. A man stood behind the glass counter, his hand on the large wooden cash register. He pushed it shut and leaned into her.

"This is Yvonne, my granddaughter," she said.

He wore a gray sailor's gansey with a rolled collar and a white stripe in his knit cap. Her hand on my elbow, she pushed me forward. Her eyes stayed on him like she could bore a hole through his sweater.

"She's a good girl," she said.

I said hello and thought it odd that she would introduce me like that to a stranger. He nodded to her, and with a long up-and-down glance, he took a visual inventory of my body.

"Like I told you, she's a good girl and she's going to go to college," she added.

"Whatever you say, Mary," he replied.

"She's my granddaughter, got it? And she's going to be living with me for a while," she said. "Okay?"

"Okay, okay, Mary," he said.

She was laying an expectation on me that at the time I had no way of knowing how to get to: going to college. The force of her intention was enough for me to eventually find a way to that world beyond, a world she could only imagine.

We took the elevator to her fifth-floor apartment. The carpet in the narrow hall was vacuumed clean over the stained art deco design. My heretic crucifix earrings dangled back and forth on my ears as I walked behind her. She glanced at them when she put the key in the door, to let me know that she noticed that I had crucifixes hanging from my ears, but said nothing. The dangling crosses had been my everyday affront to my newly converted Jehovah's Witness mother, who had renounced graven images. Anyway, at nearly nineteen, I liked Jesus better as an ornament.

San Francisco's free health clinics were what brought her west from Salt Lake. None of us knew that it was too late; her uterine cancer had gone too far.

Already tiny, Grandma got smaller and smaller the sicker she got, and any bump in the cable cars sent her flying under the seat in front of us, especially when she wore the peach chiffon shifts she liked.

One day after we cleaned one of her regular Nob Hill houses, a long tenth-floor apartment that didn't look particularly dirty to me, for her patron, the Captain, she took me to an amusement park. She liked the ball-tossing games and the shooting galleries.

"Once the ball's in the air, just let it go. It doesn't matter if you hit the target. All you have to do is aim and shoot. The outcome is not up to you," she said.

There was almost nothing left of the twenty-dollar bill she earned that day cleaning the Captain's penthouse. The carnival worker lined up three balls for a quarter and knew her by her first name. Last quarter down, she handed me the balls. I threw them one after the other, missing every shot.

"It's okay," Grandma said. "Just remember to take aim and give it your best shot. That's all you ever have to do. Once it's in the air, that's all that counts. Remember the outcome is not up to you. The game is in here, she pointed to her chest. Not out there" she said. Wisdom from my hooker come Zen Master granny.

The backdrop of broken bulbs, the too-big smiles on the fat lady tent, and the empty Ferris wheel going round and round behind us, we walked to the bus stop. I could see our bus coming in the distance, and if we ran, we could make it.

"Hurry, Grandma," I said. "Our bus is coming."

She walked at her own pace, one size-4 foot in front of the other.

"Hurry, Grandma!" I said. I raised my left hand up to the bus, my right hand open to her. "If we hurry, we can make that bus," I said louder.

She kept to her pace.

I rolled my hand to her in a speed-up circle. "I'll stop the bus." I rolled my hand faster. "Hurry!" I said.

In her slow, steady procession, she did not change her pace. "If you stop the bus, I won't get on it," she told me.

I turned in a pivot on the gravel. "What? Hurry!"

Her tiny feet stopped in the dirt. "I said if you stop that bus, I won't get on it," she repeated.

I slapped my hands against my hips and turned to face her. "Why?" I asked.

She took her last steps to the bus bench. I leaned against the wood-slat back of the bus bench and waited for her to catch up. The bus wheeled dust and dirt on me as it rolled by. She lifted herself up to the spot I'd cleared for her at the edge of the bench. Her hands over her lap, she smoothed her skirt.

"Never run after a bus," she said. She pulled her hanky out of her sleeve. The pink crochet edging unfolded in her lap as she pressed it flat. "Because, just like a man, if you wait long enough, another one will come along."

I curled my sleeve in my hand to wipe the soot off my face. "What?" I said. "What, Grandma?"

"I said men are like buses; they will come and go. Let them," she said.

"Okay, Grandma. But what if that's the last bus?"

"It's never the last bus," she said. She dabbed her forehead with the corner of her hanky. "Think about it. The last bus ever?"

I lifted my sleeve to my nose and wiped. "But Grandma, what if it's the last bus for the night?" I asked.

She put her hanky in her lap and folded it so that one corner met the other. "Sometimes it's hard. But you won't die," she replied.

My sleeves hung below my wrists, and I wiped them on the sides of my hips. I saw that I couldn't win. "Okay, Grandma," I said.

It was no use when she got into teaching mode. She pushed her hanky back into her sleeve.

There we sat while I posed various man/bus scenarios.

"And when you do get on a bus, if it's your bus, stay on it as long as you need to and get off at your own stop," she said.

"Of course," I said. "Grandma, why would I get on a bus that's not going where I'm going?" I asked.

"Exactly," she said.

"Or why would I stay on a bus past my stop?"

"Exactly," she agreed. "Don't stay on it just for the ride, mijita It's never worth it."

"I don't get it, Grandma. Why would I ride around on random buses?" I asked. "Exactly. And when it's over, it's over," she said. "Let it be over."

I stopped looking into her eyes and followed the lines of her lips to see if by reading them I could decipher what code she was speaking, because at the time, it seemed like simpleminded advice to me.

CHAPTER 23

MARMALADE

It was her habit to load every strip of cloth we owned from personal clothing to sheets, bedspreads, curtains, and throw rugs into grocery carts and head for the Laundromat at six in the morning on Saturdays. There we'd be, headed up from Post and Fillmore at dawn, loaded down with at least two Safeway carts full with nearly everything we owned, all sorted and ready to be washed, whether it needed it or not.

Just before the second stray cat left, Grandma Mary had become too weak to load the carts, so visits to the laundry got fewer and fewer. I pulled down the last of her new sheets to make her bed. By then, all she could do was move from her bed to the kitchen table.

She cut thick toast out of French bread, and I baked it in the broiler of the apartment-size four-burner gas stove. Toast lines darkened the bread on one side, then on the other side under the broiler. She pointed to one of the rich-people jars she'd brought home from one of her clients' kitchens. The jam was at the very top of the Victorian scalloped cabinet, which had been painted so many times it looked like droopy pink frosting. I pulled the jar down and broke the seal to twist it open.

With real butter on the thick toasted bread and lumpy jam over all of it, Mary put our food down on the mismatched blue, red, and black printed French provincial plates she had collected from sidewalk sales and thrift stores. The glass top on the silver coffee pot slowed its rattle as she poured her coffee.

"When your mother was born," she began, "I played with her like she was a doll."

She wrapped the embroidered "new" kitchen towel around the coffee pot like a tea cozy. The kitchen towel had been wrapped in silk in a drawer with the unpolished silver.

"I was almost thirteen when she was born, and we washed outside. I wrapped your mother in blankets and put her near the fire while I washed over it," she explained. "The wash was in large tubs, and I pushed the boiling clothes with a stick that had a can nailed to it. The can had nail holes in the bottom for the water to go through. I pushed and pulled the can into the clothes to get all the dirt out. That's how I washed."

On her red-checkered tablecloth, the blue cross-stitches on the dish towel made a bluebird. It sat perched on the handle of the silver coffee pot on a black metal trivet near the window.

"Your great-grandma Mercedes's second husband, your grandpa Vidal, was your mother's father. You knew that, didn't you? Your great-grandma Mercedes was off having babies when your grandpa Vidal started coming to my room. I was eleven," she said.

My mouth filled with thick orange jam and bread, and the unfamiliar lumps of fruit felt odd in my mouth.

I kind of knew but didn't know the way you know but don't know things nobody wants you to know, things that are better left in that know/don't know place.

"He wanted to keep your great-grandma Mercedes in the big house and keep me in the 'little house,'" she said.

The grill lines on the toast crunched in my mouth. It felt like orange peel in the jam, and all I could do was chew.

"I told him no," she continued, putting more toast on my plate. "They married me off to Sam Martinez. Butter?" she asked, and spread a pat of butter on my toast.

"Your uncle Sal was born. You didn't know him. His padrino ran him over by accident at a baptism party. It just about killed me when he died. I was fourteen," she said. She tipped the blue-bird into her red print cup. "Then Sam got deported for killing a man who tried to rob the restaurant." She spooned sugar from the minuet-print sugar bowl. "I saw the shooting from where we lived on top of the restaurant," she said. She stirred a small stream of milk into her cup. "Your uncle was born, and with Sam gone, I had to go to work."

The only thing I could see on the table was the jar, an orange on the picture of the fancy jam. It said *Marmalade.*

AS SHE NEARED THE LAST NIGHT of her life, Grandma Mary had started calling out more often at night. I was the only one there after the last regular man left. When the food she cooked for him ran out and she couldn't haul cat food up the steps anymore, he left with the stray cat.

Now when she called, she usually wanted water or for me to shift her pillow or to bring her a blanket, but mostly she wanted to know I was there. On the last night of her life, she called me.

"Yvonne."

Not Ivana.

"Yvonne."

"What, Grandma?"

I pulled the blankets over me on the hard green divan that we had lugged in the grocery cart from the Salvation Army.

"Go back to sleep," I said. "I'm here. Just go back to sleep."

I tossed and turned in the bed my uncle said we paid too much for, the bed that was so hard it made for little sleep. In my half sleep, I was back at home where Mother had taken the doorknob off my bedroom door.

I'd put a chair under the doorknob hole and spread across my bed with a deck of cards to lay out a game of solitaire. Mother patrolled the hall outside my room. I remember Grandma Mary saying not to skip a play and not to cheat, because a lie was still a lie even if only you knew it.

"I told you not to close this door," Mother said.

I ignored her and unfolded the game.

"I told you to leave this door open," she repeated.

Her voice got louder. Queen, Jack, Ten of Spades, one by one, the cards landed on my lavender ruffled bedspread. The canopy over my bed made it feel like a clubhouse. Grandma's game.

Mother forced her way into my room and shoved the chair, pushing her back against the door to block me from leaving. I faced her, put my hands on the legs of the chair, and pushed her and the chair back.

"I'm not afraid of you anymore," I said.

My foot was on the now-fallen Queen of Spades. We stood facing each other, our hands on either side of the chair. I pushed her and the chair farther back. She let go and nearly ran out of the room.

"Wait until your father gets home," she told me.

"He's not my father," I said.

I woke up and pulled the covers back to get out of bed.

"Gran," I called to her from the next room, reaching up from my hard Salvation Army bed.

She'd managed to pull a sheet down over her before she fell off the bed. That's when I found her.

CHAPTER 24

COFFEE

Thirty years after I left Utah, I was back in Salt Lake on a family visit. My kids were tired of seeing relatives, so I went alone to visit my aunt Annie. When I got there her daughter, my cousin Marian, had just gotten out of prison and was in the kitchen on the phone trying to hook up a date with her man. The long black phone cord stretched from her ear across her children's plates in the tiny kitchen, over the eggs she fried that were still bubbling from the pan. I took a seat and moved my chair in closer to them as we sat together around the table.

With the phone balanced between her ear and shoulder, my cousin made open plans for a drug hookup and a date. She spooned freshly mashed and fried beans next to the kids' eggs. Tortillas were laid in the middle of the table. She took a freshly heated tortilla, burnt just right, tore it in half, and pushed it on my plate. The phone back on the wall, she slapped the kids on the back of the heads for crying and scooted in closer to her own plate at the table. Our eyes met. She locked my gaze and said, "I take drugs because I like to get high."

It was the longest, truest gaze I ever held with her. There was nothing else to say.

"You got a problem with that? Tough shit," she added.

I stabbed my egg yolk with the torn tortilla and cut my egg into pieces.

My aunt, her mother, was in the living room. My cousin's eldest son was on the couch in front of the TV and didn't want to eat.

My aunt took her slipper off her foot and smacked the boy hard across the back of his head. Surprised out of his TV trance, he looked startled but refused to cry. So she smacked him harder and harder, the flat heel against his head, until he did. It was like the cartoons he watched, slaps, punches, and smacks, only this was real.

The look of pain, embarrassment, and resolve on his face felt familiar. It wasn't a surprise to him. It looked like he kind of expected it. Almost as if to offer me something to blunt the shock of her commonplace beating of her grandson, my aunt motioned me over to her white wicker sofa.

I finished my egg and took my coffee.

"I know what happened to Mom," she said, referring to Grandma Mary.

The boy's eyes carried his share of hate as he made his way to the seat I'd vacated at the kitchen table.

My aunt rolled her bare feet under her, shoeless from the beating she'd just administered.

"We work hard to put food on this table. Goddamn spoiled brat," she said.

I took my place in the matching wicker chair opposite her.

"Since you came all this way and been asking about your grandma, I'll tell you what she told me. If you really want to know, I'll tell you," she said.

I took a sip of my coffee and wasn't sure if I wanted to stay or leave. I put the cup down on the wicker armrest.

My aunt took that as a yes.

"Your grandma was drinkin' heavy one day when I was home hidin' from the truant officer. She was drinkin' real heavy. When she was drinkin' heavy like that, she liked to talk. That's when she said it. That's when she told me what happened to her. She was drinkin' and cryin' like she could do when she was drinkin' heavy," she explained.

"'When I was a little girl,' she said, 'my mother kept me locked up in a room. There were men lined up outside. They came in one after another and got on top of me. It hurt so bad. I cried and cried for her to stop them. Oh God, it hurt so bad,' she said.

"'She never did,' your grandma Mary said. "Your great-grandma Mercedes just stood outside the door and took the money."

My coffee lay on my tongue like it didn't know which way to go, just lie there or get swallowed.

CHAPTER 25

SAINT MARY IN BLUE INK

There were two services when my mother died, one for the Saved and one for the Damned.

She was sixty when she died of a stroke. It was the spring of 1995.

The Damned were ushered to special box seats under swags of red velvet where we could see but not participate in the service for her conducted by the Saved.

There were no statues of any kind or colored glass windows or candles or gold water bowls for dipping, crossing, or kneeling. The funeral hall was full and notable only for the sound of pages turning. From our alcove we witnessed wave after wave of page turning. Pages of scripture flipped back and forth from John to Luke, to Paul, and back again. But for the novice page turners, who were a few black-ink-on-rice-paper pages behind, the page turning would have been the same.

Back and forth, there were pages to celebrate. Pages to extol. Pages to proclaim the dead not dead. There was no grief; no one in Mother's huge community of church people wailed. They found solace and comfort in their belief that our mother had simply left the body she had inhabited for sixty years. The body in the closed black box in the front of the room was hers, but she wasn't dead.

We marveled at the rate at which the Saved found their references and the ease at which they found their refuge. Led by my brother, the seventh son, there was no reason to cry, no reason to grieve, and most of all, no reason to be sad; our mother had simply just left her body and was now finally free.

She was not only free from her body. She was free from the burden of our salvation. Some of us had chosen or had been forced to choose her God; the rest of us had not, or would not. When Mother found "The Truth," it was her answer for everything. It was her answer for all the years of abuse and neglect. If we would now just join her, we would be saved too and be able to join her in the "New Kingdom." It was our fault, we the refusers, if after all she had done for us in finding "Jehovah," we wouldn't receive "Jehovah" like she had. She had found his love, and now was on her way. On her way to wait for "The Call" to the "New System."

And to wait for us once we were ready to join her there.

We all did still have a chance to see our mother again, if we wanted, but only if we found our way to her God, only to her God and only by her way to him.

Now it would be her turn to wait.

Jehovah or no Jehovah, we had already become used to wanting and waiting for what we needed from our mother. It was our ache for her that made it real. If we couldn't have what we needed from her, then we would have the pain of not having it. We built our own emotional shrines to that ache. No, we built basilicas to it. Story after story of want, need, slight, deprivation, and abandonment was our offering.

Now there could be no more offerings to our basilica of hurt.

In this final abandonment, our church went empty.

The Catholic ladies from our block showed up at our mother's service for the Saved. Since Mother's conversion, the ladies, like some of her children, had been relegated to the "World," the place where "Worldliness" led to rampant misdeeds that kept you from God. So like us, the ladies had become untouchable yet worthy of saving if only they, too, like us, could see their way to Mother's God.

In response to Mother's efforts to convert them, the ladies began to post notices on their front doors to declare their homes to be Catholic homes. Solicitors, especially Mother and her converts, were not welcome. The ladies chose the Virgin Mary in blue ink for their stick-on door postings. No other faiths were welcome, so declared the benevolent Virgin in blue italic letters, her arms spread wide, her palms open. "That means you." The thin glue-back sheets were everywhere, on front doors, garages, mailboxes, and even on doghouses. The ladies chose St. Mary to make their point, not La Virgen de Guadalupe. It was more formal that way, in English. No mercy. No backsliding. No intercession.

Undeterred by the postings even after her stroke, Mother was committed to covering her territory and to logging her hours to find new converts. She dragged her silver walker past home after home of blue St. Mary postings. Fewer and fewer unposted houses were left in the immediate neighborhood, so her route got wider and farther, making it even more difficult for her to reach her required number of contacts. Unfazed, Mother rolled her silver walker up and down the hills of Boyle Heights, with the City of Los Angeles as her backdrop. She rolled past the panaderías, past laundromats where she left her magazines, past the projects, past the closed-off freeway tunnels and halfway to the monolith Sears building and back.

Florence Samaniego walked up the middle aisle at the service for the Saved. Page turners on each side of her, Florence paused without kneeling before entering her pew. Her petite frame upright and her tiny brown hands folded in her lap, she sat in stillness amid the page turners. Her head uncovered, she held no beads but wore a gold crucifix around her neck.

Tiny with dark skin and short salt-and-pepper hair, Florence made a dent in the sea of page turning. She represented the half dozen mothers on our block, who, like Mother, had raised Catholic-sized families in the tiny bungalows in the hills just southeast of the city.

Florence and her family of nine lived two houses down the block from our family of eleven. Before Mother's conversion, we'd played and gone to Catholic school with her kids.

Florence's mother lived across the street from us in a big yellow well-kept house that had the only usable football lawn. Theirs was one of the few families left on the block after the Santa Ana Freeway was built through the neighborhood, cutting it in half. The block went up for sale, and we were able to buy the one-bedroom bungalow lodged with theirs between the new freeway and the projects.

We hardly ever saw Florence's mother and only knew her as Florence's mother. She lived with her adult son, Florence's brother, whose name we didn't know either. We knew him as Johnnie's uncle. Black lunch bucket in hand, he wore the same gray uniform to work every day. Only Florence came and went to her mother's yellow house.

The day Florence's mother died, it was before Mother's stroke and Mother knew of it in the way that she sometimes knew things that nobody told her. She looked out our bay window to the yellow house, walked back to the kitchen, and gathered her dish-wet hands in the blue cornflowers of her apron to dry them. She pulled it off her neck and hung the apron on the nail that held up the Union Pacific Railroad calendar. She smoothed her hair back and put on the only makeup she ever wore, her red lipstick, and went across the street to the yellow house.

Mother walked up the concrete steps past the dried flower urns and the brown lawn to knock on the screen door. The screen door opened, a little at first, then wider, and then wide enough for Mother to walk into the yellow house right past the blue virgin posting. Florence led Mother upstairs to where her dead mother lay. Mother sat with Florence on the edge of the bed and waited with her until the coroner came. Florence's hands in my mother's hands. No words between them.

I pulled back the red velvet curtains from where we had been seated to find my way to Florence amid the page turners.

"Mrs. Samaniego," I said. My tears welled up and were ready to make their own offering of grief. "It's so good to see you."

I reached to touch her but was stopped by a hand at my elbow. I turned to see my stepfather.

"Wha' so matta?" he asked.

His white shirt stiff against his brown neck, his tie didn't match his overstuffed suit.

"Jue mader ees happy now," he said.

Once an impeccable dresser, his clothes stopped matching when he got saved. He got close enough to whisper to me, his mustache clipped neat against his upper lip.

"Don' cry," he said. "Dis is wha jue mader wan."

I stopped at the edge of the pew and could feel myself stifle a sob. My heave went back inside all the way down my throat. He was right. This is what Mother wanted. To be dead in her body and alive where we couldn't reach her, where nobody could reach her. I stepped past him and sat next to Florence at the edge of her pew. She held my hands in her tiny brown hands, and we sat together with only the sound of pages turning around us.

In her way, Mother's final act, her letting go of the life she had for the one she believed waited for her in the "New System," was, as I see it now, a principled and courageous act.

CHAPTER 26

HASTA LA VICTORIA SIEMPRE

In May of 1980 I was led out of Schmitz Hall in hand cuffs at the University of Washington in Seattle. Front page coverage in the University newspaper, *The Daily*, reported over a hundred of us, a coalition of Black, Latino, Asian, Native American and poor white students had shut down the university administration building.

Under pressure from upper class white parents, the university had threatened to limit admission to poor students and students of color who'd gained admission through the EOP (Educational Opportunity Program) using the Allen Bakke reverse discrimination case as a pretext.

The underlying assumption driving the university's push was that we were ill prepared to attend the prestigious University of Washington because EOP students dropped out at higher rates than general admission students, therefore reserving limited spaces for us was denying spaces to "more deserving" general admission students.

Chicano graduate researchers drew a different conclusion— in fact they found the recidivism rate for our cohort was much lower than for general admission students. When pressed for additional research data to buttress their findings, the university refused to provide it.

Our tactical goal in the planned action that led up to the mass arrests was to get into the university president's office and take it over. We devised various routes to get past the guards to get to the top floor where his office was. Two of us almost made it. We got there and I literally got my foot in the door when campus security pushed the door against my foot so hard that I had to pull it out. I was then escorted downstairs where over a hundred of us had taken over the lobby and had been holding it for hours with a plan to stay overnight and for as long as it took. Some of our professors brought our classes to the takeover.

The campus police started with mock arrests. Several groups had been handcuffed taken outside and released, not arrested. When the handcuffed group I was with got to the front doors of administration building, the released group outside yelled at us to "Go back, go back." We went back inside. "Now you're really under arrest," the campus police said. They tightened our plastic cuffs and packed us into police vans to take us to the King County Jail.

When we got to the jail, the men were sent one way and women sent to another. We stuck together as much as we could. María Rosa, a member of MUJER, a Latina campus-based organization, had a beautiful singing voice and sang *De Colores* loud enough for us to hear her throughout the jail. We joined in song so she could hear us and so we could hear each other. We made a tally of who we could identify and called out for who we didn't hear from.

When the largest group of us got to our cell we were met with the leader of the women already in the cell. She had her flank behind her as we entered, cell door shut behind us. Remembering the respect etiquette protocols from neighborhood street encounters back home, I assured her we were not there to take over the cell or challenge their cell turf in anyway. We were college students only there for a night. We worked out toilets, sinks, and bunks. The only thing we wanted I told her was to watch the five o'clock news because we'd just shut down the university's administration building and wanted to see the coverage. At mealtime, we got a green salad. I took a bite and tasted only oil on the limp oily leaves. No vinegar.

"Keep your clothes on," the cell women told us. Sure enough, male guards made it a point to walk the plank between the cell blocks more often than usual.

"Why so many visits?" one of the women called out to the guards. "Trying to get a peek at the college girls, you assholes? You never visit us this many times. Isn't my ass good enough?" She pulled down her pants to reveal a butt cheek. We just sat there clutching our blankets. The other women laughed.

We gathered around the five o'clock news only to see a news bulletin that Mount St. Helens had just erupted. People were missing in the lava's path and there was ash everywhere. We watched the entire hour all the way down to the last story, fixing our eyes to the bottom of the screen to see if a piece of our story would eke out. Nothing. Nobody was interested in arrested college students. After months of planning and organizing and our campaign was eclipsed by a volcano.

We got out and dug out from the volcanic ash that covered everything and retooled our campaign to target finals and graduation. One tactic was to glue the cards in the card catalogues together in key libraries so they were stuck together and unusable, thereby crippling main research arteries before finals. It was a simple discreet tactic that we could do all at once with minimum risk. Ultimately, we were able to negotiate an agreement with the university before graduation to protect the EOP program. The university didn't want to find out what we had planned to greet parents and families with at graduation.

MY ROAD TO THE U OF W WAS not a straight line. I barely graduated from high school. My first husband was a Black man, one of the many Black families who settled in Boyle Heights from East Texas. We met on the Roosevelt High School track field, I ran the mile and he threw the shot put and javelin. We had a journalism class together. He and his brother were LA All City Football Players of the Year. I was on the drill team, a Roosevelt Riderette.

I knew my parents would never let me date him because he was Black. After dating furtively for months, we went to grad night together at Disneyland, the night of our high school graduation.

When he moved up to Washington State to find his father, I followed him there and helped him pursue his college football dream. I wrote the letters that got him into WSU Washington State University in Pullman, Washington. I eventually joined him with our baby daughter and got a clerical job in the Military Science Department. Where I came from this job was an achievement, relatively good paying professional work with benefits. My baby was in daycare and my jock husband was taking art classes and working out. One of my job benefits allowed me to audit classes for free. The mystique of collegiate intellectual unattainability was broken when I met PhD students. I can do this, I remember thinking. This was new territory, nobody in my family had ever broken ground in this world.

Down the hall from my Military Science job was the Chicano Student Counseling Center. Chicano students were in and out of the center all day having been admitted to WSU from all over the country. The center was a hub where students met to discuss lectures, issues, build community, laugh, tell stories and sing corridos. Guitarists, poets, painters, science and social science nerds of all kinds met there. A whole world opened up. Pretty soon I was at the center at all my breaks and started to join student activities on weekends. What I hated most about my job was having to wait until 5 p.m. to go home even when my work was all done. Missing my baby for those hours was miserable, but the money was steady. When I picked her up from the Indian family who took care of her for me, her hair smelled like saffron.

One day, I took a leap, quit my job, applied for loans and with the Chicano Student Counseling Center's help enrolled as a full-time student through the EOP. I could spend more time with my baby, develop my mind and join a movement. It was exciting.

Pretty soon there were study groups at our house; and poker game fundraisers conducted by my husband, who sat our daughter on his lap, put a visor on her, put cards in her tiny hands, and made her the dealer. We also had political meetings to strategize around campus issues.

One of the first actions we organized was the takeover of the WSU student newspaper to protest a racist cartoon showing EOP students being flushed down a toilet. We got into the newsroom and typewriters were about to start flying out the window when the editor came out and wanted to talk.

Before going into negotiations, I remember turning to look at the students who had gathered behind us before a smaller group of us went in to the meeting with the editor and staff. To a person, the students said, "You can do it. We know you can. We're behind you." I remember the fear, the excitement and the real desire not to let them down. We negotiated a deal for improved coverage of our issues and we developed longstanding ties with the newsroom staff.

As my political awareness grew, I focused my studies on the global class based political divide. I was elected MECHA (Movimiento Estudiantil Chicano De Aztlan) president, a Chicano student political organization. I won by a very few votes. In a brawl between left and right factions, that led up to my election, one of our comrades got jumped by the reactionaries. He got bruised and battered but never backed down. He was the brother of a university professor from East Texas, whose accent was so thick, I could hardly understand him at first. I'll never forget Dave Camacho.

My husband's college football career faltered, but he became engrossed in his art and drawing classes. His sketches were everywhere. I wish I'd kept some of them. I joined a Mexican folkloric group to celebrate my newfound love for Mexican culture. A major departure from the assimilationist pedagogy I was raised in. Soon enough we were in two different worlds. Not long after, I ran for and won a seat on the student council.

My brother remarked our house was like a scene from the movie *The Way We Were*. I was organizing and leading political rallies and my husband was at the basketball court or at the art studio. I looked for him at all the rallies and actions we organized, but would never find him there.

We were very far apart from the night he asked me to marry him. That night I wore a red velvet long dress and my first pregnancy had started to show. It was a clear, starry, dark blue night and the moon was full. I said yes. We took out a marriage license, but never had the ceremony because we were too broke to buy rings.

One day he took the car and left Pullman for Seattle to get a "real job" he said. He was tired of being broke. I was left with, by then, two babies. We made efforts at reconciliation. I'd get rides to Seattle with the kids and he'd come to Pullman, usually to get money until I stopped payment on the checks he snuck out of my checkbook and wrote to himself. I also stopped payment on the car when he sent no money. In one last effort to save the marriage, I decided to move to Seattle with the kids. He wanted me to quit school and get a job. I said I would transfer to the University of Washington to finish my degree. I managed the transfer with the help of the Chicano Student Counseling Center who also helped me arrange for housing and daycare in Seattle at the University of Washington.

When I got to the Seattle Greyhound bus station, kids in tow, he was nowhere to be found. I called a friend who was living there. She helped me get settled in to the empty university student housing apartment. The housing caretaker helped me pull together beds, tables, and chairs. I got the kids into the campus daycare and enrolled in classes. Off and on over my time there, three of my brothers came to help me. One brother sent me money for a car. I will always be grateful to them for that.

I resumed my life as an activist, joined MUJER, a campus-based Latina women's group in Seattle. We joined forces in the Anti Bakke reverse discrimination fight to save the EOP from the University of Washington's plan to cut it. These actions led to my arrest the day volcano erupted.

As many of us got closer to graduation, MUJER started to transition its activism to community social services. We got grants to do housing advocacy and were temporarily housed at El Centro de la Raza, a storied Seattle Chicano community organization. There was a dispute and they tried to evict us. I remember standing in the doorway when the director tried to forcibly gain entry. When I wouldn't move, he backed away. This was one time when all those beatings I took came in handy. I wasn't afraid of physical violence.

We eventually moved our small advocacy office to a new location, in of all places, White Center, Washington. My student loans exhausted, my husband gone again, I had to go to work so I left the university 10 credits short of a degree. The MUJER Housing Program hired me and it was there that I began to learn the advocacy skills that prepared me for my later work as a paralegal and eventually as a labor negotiator and organizer. Irene Gutierrez, a legal advocate who worked there coached me and walked me through the administrative hearing process. I got my first caseload.

MUJER members were recruited travel to Cuba as part of the Venceremos Brigade, a Cuban solidarity group. There were twelve members in our Seattle based contingent, composed of students, academics, and community activists from all over the Pacific Northwest. I was designated the Travel *Responsable*, the travel leader for our group. Brigadistas from all over the US and the world traveled to Cuba to support the Cuban Revolution. The US travel blockade meant the only way to get to Cuba was through Mexico or Canada. We would travel through Montreal. We spent weeks preparing for the trip and raised our own travel funds. My children were cared for by other MUJER members while I was away.

The night before our flight to Montreal we were driven around in circles in a caravan until we landed at a MUJER member's small one-bedroom apartment. The twelve of us slept on the floor wherever we could. We were given instructions not to speak to anyone at the airport. If we recognized anyone or if someone tried to talk to us, we were instructed to fall asleep, sitting or standing.

I alone was given the information for our contact who would meet us at the Montreal airport, and a phone number to call only as a last resort in case of trouble. At Sea-Tac while we waited for our flight, I saw my best friend from high school. The fall asleep instructions gave way to the impulse to greet my friend. When I remembered my fall asleep instructions, I told her I couldn't talk, but that I was in the Seattle phonebook. We said good-bye and never saw each other again.

The person the Brigade sent to accompany us at Sea-Tac wore a large trench coat and a wide brimmed hat that he bent to try to hide his face. His outfit was more conspicuous than we all were. Finally boarded, we got to Montreal, where we were to meet our next contact. The instructions were not clear—were we to meet the contact before or after customs? Was our contact, like us, traveling on the plane or beyond the customs gate? I held us back until our group came under the notice of the customs police. We were sequestered, questioned, our passports taken and told we would have to spend the night at a Holiday Inn. The Holiday Inn turned out to be an immigration jail in a hotel with no doors. There were only people of color in the detention center dining area. Our suitcases were searched by a large matron who shouted commands at us in French. We were separated and I was placed in a room with a woman who came in as a detainee, but was there ostensibly to question me. I made the call that morning.

While waiting, we, those of us who know how to, spoke to each other in Caló described as a Mexican underworld argot, so that no one else could understand us. We were released in enough time to catch the second weekly Cubana Airlines flight to Havana. A day later, and we would have missed the last flight of the week and our trip would have been aborted. While we waited, I asked one of our group to type a report we created about what had happened to us and to make a copy of it. One copy of the report was for the Cuban *Responsable* when we got there. The other copy I hid in the lining of my suitcase.

At Jose Martí International Airport in Havana we were greeted by a cheering crowd as heroes who had defied the imperialists. It didn't feel right, we weren't heroes so much as we were given bad contact information; our travel contact had failed to inquire about us once we were detained.

We were taken to Campo Antonio Maceo, a camp for Brigadistas and other internationalists. The camp was a former plantation with still yielding groves. Antonio Maceo was a Black war hero in the war against Spain. As we settled in, we learned to watch out for white frogs that jumped at us in the toilet stalls. We learned to love pork, Cuban coffee, black beans and rice, also known as Christianos y Moros, Christians and Moors, Cuban rum, and nightly tardeadas where we were served aguas frescas fresh juices of watermelon and other fruits. We learned not to send any clothes with buttons on them to be laundered. The clothing came back buttonless. Compañera, I was told, this is the impact of underdevelopment. My copy of the report we created in Montreal went missing too. Someone had removed it from my suitcase lining.

For the first time in my life, I could be inconspicuous. I could walk among other brown and Black people unnoticed without feeling the need to guard or explain myself. It was true liberation. We met the Cuban Olympic team; a Black woman javelin medalist greeted us. She was pregnant and in training. I saw in her an indescribable radiance as she discussed her sport and her role as an athlete in the Cuban Revolution. When she spoke about her work as a revolutionary and the support she got as a woman and mother, she commanded a presence of wholeness, commitment and purpose. It was so inspiring, I wept.

We climbed the Escambray Mountains, where the water was so pure I could not drink enough of it. Our destination was the camp where Fidel and Che based their campaign against Fulgencio Bautista, the corrupt Cuban president. We saw their camp headquarters, living quarters, classrooms, an outside amphitheater, and hospital where the revolutionaries trained and took refuge in their six-year campaign to overthrow the Bautista government.

I met my second husband, a white man, on this trip, he had joined our brigade from Oregon. We first held hands at a rally in Havana. One night we skipped one of Fidel's televised speeches and went to Mango Lane, a famous lovers' getaway. We declared ourselves to the Revolution and to each other. When we got back to the camp, Fidel was still making one of his famous three-hour speeches. He didn't tell me he was still involved with another woman back in Oregon and that he had an STD. Our marriage ended years later when he became involved with another woman. It ended how it began, with deception and manipulation.

MY FIRST JOB AFTER COLLEGE WAS in a Legal Aid office, a not-for-profit poverty law firm in Portland, Oregon. They needed a Spanish-speaking person to represent the large number of Cubans who had left the island. Fidel referred to them as escoria, scum. My facility with Cuban Spanish came in handy, and the skills I learned from work with Irene at MUJER were invaluable. The Legal Aid case meetings were led by staff attorneys and held partly in Yiddish. Thankfully, my kind and caring mother-in-law gave me a copy of *The Joys of Yiddish* as a holiday gift.

"So, the guy got fired for schtupping the help," would be the beginning line of an employment law case discussion. I'd pull out *Joys of Yiddish* to find the word, trying to find the spelling, *Sch* or *sht* until I got to it. "Oooh, I said. "Got it." A new word for having sex with someone. And so it went, my Yiddish vocabulary grew exponentially, and it comes in handy to this day. It was during that time that I was able to finish my U of W degree through extended learning.

My rank-and-file union experience started in this job. The boss was an asshole and was sleeping with the office manager. More than one staff attorney could be found weeping at her desk because of his abuse. Worst of all, our pay was so low, we were eligible for public assistance. And, we learned the director was hoarding a substantial reserve. We organized a union and affiliated with National Organization of Legal Service Workers, UAW, AFL-CIO. We had occasional assistance from a traveling rep, but mostly we had to bargain our first contract ourselves.

Because Legal Aid was a nonprofit, they got pro bono help from the city's big dog downtown management law firms. In those days you could literally blow smoke at each other across the bargaining table. That's how I learned how to bargain contracts. I made every novice mistake, but nothing was lost; my skills expanded. It took us years of bargaining and finally a direct-action campaign targeting the Multnomah County Courthouse led by my colleague and fellow paralegal Cliff Jones to get a us our first contract. The result in increased pay was dramatic and we were protected from the indiscriminate whims of a tyrant. He left soon after we signed the contract. I remember singing "Ding dong, the witch is dead," down the hallway the day I heard he was gone, only to be shushed by some of my still shaken colleagues. I sang anyway.

I saw the departed director years later at a social event and thanked him being an asshole, but for that I wouldn't have learned how to fight and organize and do the work I loved as a labor negotiator and organizer. He laughed and said "You're welcome."

CHAPTER 27

WHITHER THE TROLL?
AN ORGANIZER'S TALE

*"The mode of being of the new intellectual can no longer
consist in eloquence . . . but in active participation
in practical life, as constructor, organizer, 'permanent
persuader' and not just a simple orator . . . "*
                                                    —ANTONIO GRAMSCI

Neck sweat on my black leather shoulder strap, I balanced
a briefcase on my hip to manage the rolls of butcher paper
and a handful of markers stuck in the side of it. I walked
past the community laundromat where the locals, baskets in
hand, walked in and out of a cracked and duct-taped windowed
door that was propped open by somebody's wadded-up and
discarded underwear. Their arms stretched over a car hood,
others balanced cigarettes hanging from their mouths. Some
just sat catatonic in front of the tumble dry. There was a FOR
RENT sign in the brown tinted window next door to where I was
headed. I was going to meet the committee.

My red lipstick got sucked into my lips, and my lungs worked extra hard to pull in breath when I walk in.

I laid my briefcase on the fake wood table and pushed back a chair in the community room. My nude sheer-to-toe stockings snagged close to a tear from the exposed underside of the round table. Hunched over, I pulled out pressboard splinters from my knee. My black heels pointed toe to toe into a square of industrial green linoleum.

Steamy yellow curry in Tupperware, a brown bread sandwich in wax paper, half of last night's enchilada on a paper plate, and something macrobiotic from the microwave completed their circle. The committee was made up of the four clinicians, down from eight, who treated the city's poor, elderly, and mentally ill.

They were stressed to the limit of their clinical capacities and collegial therapist civility. Led by a Quaker who needed crutches to walk, they were a nurse who spoke in very soft, almost inaudible tones; a social worker in her last trimester of pregnancy; and another social worker whose hands were bound. Volunteers answered the phones since downtown decided to starve the clinic by not filling positions.

Nobody knew where the missing positions were. Their secret codes and the terms of their release in the form of job postings were known only to the elusive troll whose offices nobody could find and who owed allegiance to no one. Nobody ruled the troll, not the local elected supervisor, not the mayor, and certainly not the dozens of mid-level bureaucrats whose job it was to confound the city's frontline workers.

Downtown had killed city civil service jobs and replaced them with contract workers who had no civil service protection or benefits. These contract workers became the virtual slaves of the system. They were at-will employees, which meant they could be fired without cause, and they had no benefits. They were abetted by the nefarious business community's front that operated under the misnomer the Committee on Jobs, whose goal it was to privatize all city work in order to restore patronage, reward friends, and silence activists. Patronage jobs were exempt from civil service vetting and usually filled by friends or patrons of elected officials, and others typically not required to go through a qualification process. Civil service systems were set up to provide for objective vetting systems, such as qualifications testing and objective qualifications review, and were put in place as way to staunch racist and sexist exclusions in public sector jobs.

Huddled together and barely speaking to one another, the clinic workers decided to call the union. Calling the union sometimes meant seeing what favors could be pulled to appease the troll—the indulgent, fickle troll.

Since I hadn't been there long enough to shore up any favors, the beleaguered outpost had little to expect from me. But they were desperate.

New to these particular turf battles, I had only what I have always had, my very own blueprint for a fight, which I adapted from Harvard academics Fisher and Ury's book entitled *Getting to Yes*. I'd met them in Cambridge at the Harvard Trade Union Program where I was a national fellow.

Mine was the "Homey D. Clown" version, "Getting to Yes or Kicking Your Ass," a method of engagement used successfully in all kinds of situations, from a five-person group of organized middle managers to a several-thousand-member group of county workers and everything in between, public and private.

"Give me an hour tops," I told the committee. "In one hour, we will have a game plan. Just get the key players together near a wall."

First, to use Fisher and Ury's methodology, the problem was framed in the form of a question.

"So, what is the question?" I asked the committee.

They looked at me like, "*The question?*" *What do you think the question is? We're dying here. No secretary, no email, down four therapists, and dealing with all these crazy old people. What the fuck do you think the question is?*"

In my best adapted therapist tone, I told them it was important that we agreed on what this fight was about so that we could formulate a strategy.

"OKAAYYY . . ." they said after serious cross-glancing at each other.

"How can we provide the best services to our clients?" the Quaker said.

"How's that?" They all leaned toward me over their food.

"Good enough," I said.

Feeling like the umpteenth idiot trainer, I moved on, forgoing the deeper discussion that would tell me more about who they were and what they cared about. I would learn what I had to learn in battle.

The next question in the Getting-to-Yes process was "What's the data?"

Done right, it would lead to a discussion to find what the Cubans would call "La Conjunctura." Harkening Fidel, it was the point at which this battle located itself in the context of the overall struggle to end capitalist domination, right here, right now at the Southeast Mission Geriatric Mental Health Clinic in San Francisco, the home of the free clinic movement.

In short, what were the numbers? What was the census? How long had there been vacancies? What was the billing data? Who were our allies? What were the stories? How could we document the impact of the city's neglect on the elderly, poor, and mentally ill? How could we quantify it in real terms? Who had the power to get us what we wanted? What politicians could we embarrass or help?

This was also where the data not immediately available would get tasked out. Who could get what? When could we get it? This was a key part to this process, because as the committee began to collectively see what they had, they started to analyze the problem organically in their own terms.

When they started to get focused on the larger array of their strengths and not just where they were stuck, they took own-ership of the problem and moved away from the "You're the union, you fix it" approach of "That's what we pay you for . . ."

By now we had a volunteer scribe. We had formed the question and figured out what we did and did not know. The butcher paper started to fill up. Here is where I told them about their legal rights to their growing information request. That I would draft the request to track the labor law to set up a parallel litigation track as needed. Unfair labor practice charges are useless, but they can be used as a propaganda tool for further escalation. This also signaled to the boss that we were serious and we knew what we were talking about.

As a legal worker, I can tell you, it's important to know the law, but any successful organizer will tell you the real power is in organizing. The law is just backup.

The third key step in the problem-solving process was brainstorming, prefaced by basic ground rules: no judging, no comments, and no evaluation. You just had to get it up there and see what stuck. Anything was allowed. Cutting loose, wild, crazy ideas, whatever.

The temptation here was to figure it out for them. The hardest and by far best thing to do, though, was to wait. To let what was organically theirs emerge. It could be hell for a fixer not to fix. For a rescuer not to rescue. For a know-it-all not to give the answer. Hellish though it may be, it was always worth the wait. When you got to that "tipping point," it was the best part of the work.

As the butcher paper filled up with ideas, the discussion was instructive and lively. In this Freirean moment, the dialectic shifted and the teacher became the learner. The job here was to listen, probe, challenge, agitate, bait, cajole, and tell stories about actions taken by other workers, whatever it took to open to what was there. Done right, the "students" would then start to lead.

Finally, a single idea or two would break through and turn into an "action" or, in legal terms, a "concerted activity."

Ideas were then organized, categorized, and evaluated against a standard of risk and involvement. The action must be SMART: Strategic, Measurable, Accessible, Relevant, & Timely.

The developing game plan on the wall kept us all accountable and provided a way to measure progress, to make adjustments as needed, to factor in new information, and to have a document for evaluation when the campaign was over.

This was where I broke with Fisher and Ury, who go on to develop their method of consensus building in contract negotiations. In my experience, there was no will to consensus without a recognition of power. I used a truncated version of their steps to build power first. Dealing with the boss was for later.

What flowed was creative, thoughtful, and original. One group was so terrified of the boss that they couldn't agree on a slogan for a basic sticker campaign. They decided to leave their stickers blank. The blank round sticker would symbolize their muted speech.

Blank round stickers were posted everywhere, in the mail room, on the time clock, in the lunchroom, and in the bathrooms. They sent unsuspecting allies into meetings with the boss with blank stickers plastered on their chests. Predictably, the no-message message provoked even more interest than a printed one would have, and said volumes about their fear.

When it hits, it hits.

The room was full at the staff meeting where the blank sticker workers had organized themselves into an "action" orchestrated to silently confront the boss. It was enough to get that boss to cave.

Although at first these actions seem small, they are prized by *The Art of War* author, Chinese general Sun Tzu, as incremental engagement in the periphery, providing for the widest field of action with the enemy and an opportunity for the enemy to withdraw or change position.

When workers win in this way, they do what Frantz Fanon describes as breaking the unspoken agreement with their oppressor to be complicit in their own oppression. To quote a nurse activist at a critical prestrike meeting, "No one can oppress you without your permission."

"That's right," she said to a convention hall full of Monterey County workers on the verge of a strike. "They can't," she continued, "unless you let them."

Monterey County workers, in one of many actions that led up to that strike, "cited" the errant county executive who had gotten away without a citation after breaking a parking turnstile when she tried to elude the police. The officer caught her but declined to cite her once he saw who she was.

Outraged county workers, who themselves had been written up for every imaginable infraction, organized a mass mail-in of facsimile "citations" drafted by their public defender members. They cited the county executive for evading the ticket, as well as for well-documented labor abuses and a litany of other offenses. Their leaders presented the stack of "citations" along with a large poster-size one in open session at a Monterey County Board of Supervisors meeting where they publicly cited her.

In Oakland, in another well-covered "action," parking deputies exposed a citywide pattern of racist ticketing practices, where the city dwellers in the hills in the big houses got warnings for parking infractions and poor folks in the flatlands got the tickets.

It also exposed a piece-rate contracted-out ticket adjudication system where a contract worker showed up in her pajamas to load up contested tickets in the trunk of her car to take them home to review them. Paid by the piece, how many do you think got reversed?

In small fights and big ones, workers find common ground in struggle. They find shared purpose and intimate awareness about what they endure. They treat each other differently. There is less infighting and backstabbing. More healing can happen in one day of concerted activity than in years of individual therapy.

The day the striking Multnomah County public defenders shut down the courthouse in Portland, Oregon, to protest the unequal justice system rigged to provide better pay for the lawyers who put you in jail versus the vastly lower pay for the lawyers who kept you out, there was a celebration in the park. The lawyers, their families, and their clients ate pizza and cake at a picnic on the lawn and took turns delivering speeches under a tree in front of the shut-down courthouse.

Even the rank-and-file DAs brought water out to their striking counterparts that hot day. The head DA paced in front of the shut-down courthouse and refused my hand when I offered it to him. It wasn't about him.

The SE Geriatric Clinic Committee decided to organize a noontime lunch and rally with escalation, if needed, to the display of a ten-foot banner on South Mission Avenue and, if necessary, across the street to temporarily shut down traffic.

We worked out a target number of clients and their families to turn out. Names were listed, and each member took responsibility for calling the people on their list. We met week after week to nail down commitments. We evaluated the information we got or didn't get from our information requests and sent follow-up demands.

We deliberated over food, the sound system, press releases, and outreach to sympathetic community groups. We talked about falloff. Would the falloff be higher or lower because of the particular needs of these clients, considering confidentiality issues, etc.?

We became focused on the date *we* set and removed focus from the boss, who at this point had started to focus on us.

When it hits, it really hits.

The committee's work unleashed the impact of their organizing as well as their cumulative therapeutic work with the community. What Scott Peck names as love, the "work of attention," this clinic's specific therapeutic practice was dedicated to the city's poor, elderly, and mentally ill. It was their stock and trade to listen, to attend, to help heal. This love would be the basis of their strength and the trove of their power. Now SE Geriatric clients and their families could give back.

And they did.

The community room was full. There was a purple banner on the wall that proclaimed "City Workers March for Peace and Justice," to the delight of the Quaker. On the high table that served as the podium right under the banner there were fresh orange, red, and pink roses from the nurse's garden. The husband of one of the social workers set up the sound system, and the community señoras brought in *buñuelos* and pudding. There were aluminum trays of food ordered by the union headquarters.

One of the first to arrive was a tiny gray-haired woman whose red lipstick was colored outside the lines of her mouth, one red curve above her lip and one red curve below. She snapped and unsnapped the gold-and-rhinestone clasp on her black patent leather purse and did not move from her front row seat. A man with wall-to-wall sunglasses sat in the back under the pull-down plastic shades that held up the "For Rent" sign. His glasses let nothing in. A brother and sister with ivory crucifixes large enough to rival a rap star's came in and leaned over the sign-in sheet, their alabaster Jesuses lying on the page.

A woman who could have been my mother's age walked up to me and matter-of-factly announced, "I have bipolar disorder."

"Okay," I said.

"Where should I sit?" she asked.

"Anywhere," I replied.

She walked to the window by the laundromat and back to the front door and back again before settling in the middle behind the lipstick lady.

Soon enough, there were no more chairs for the still-arriving clients and their families. Workers from other clinics showed up, as well as various community groups and the local press and radio. It was standing room only. The buzz really started up when a city official arrived, ostensibly to announce that—guess what?—the positions had been found.

"It's a miracle," someone said. *Yeah,* I thought, *like finding the Virgen de Guadalupe's image in a tortilla or a shop floor oil slick.* Might the miracle have had to do with the threat that fifty elderly mental health patients were ready to hold up a banner across Mission to ask inconvenient questions about the city's healthcare system at a time when there was national focus on it?

The committee decided to allow the city official to take the mic. But not before rousing the seniors, their families, and their supporters into a loud pledge that they would do whatever was necessary to fight for their clinic. More importantly, notwithstanding anything the city official said, they made it clear to him that he would have to answer to them. To his credit, he acknowledged that indeed, it was their activism that made the difference.

In a moment that lined up every trajectory of my political, professional, and personal life, and one that I will never forget, one of the clients got up to speak.

He was carefully shaved to sculpt the handsome lines of his deep-brown face. His salt-and-pepper hair and mustache were trimmed close. He wore a suit and a tie and could easily have passed as a history professor or a preacher. He took the mic and held it for a moment before speaking.

"I have a mental illness," he said.

He paused again.

"I have spent a large part of my life in prison," he said.

It got so quiet, all you could hear was the bus clattering up Mission through the window.

"I'm not going back," he said.

The lady with the patent leather purse snapped it shut.

"Until I came here to see Shelly, I had not been diagnosed," he continued.

Something began to roll in on me from every limb of my body.

"I am now on medication, and with the help of this clinic, I am managing my illness," he said.

And soon enough, as though a dam had burst in my head, there were tears in my eyes.

It was at that moment that I stopped thinking about new ways to find and torture the troll and the politician who couldn't bother to show up or even send someone. I laid down my I'm-in-charge-of-the-event clipboard and let myself sit with my union *comadres*: women, nurses, and activists from the union's leadership who had come out. Hardened veterans of many battles, we huddled together in our folding chairs and we wept. And we wept.

"We need this clinic," he said.

The man with the wall-to-wall glasses stuck a tissue through the side of his glasses to catch his tears.

"Are we going to let them take this clinic away from us?" the speaker asked.

The brother and sister sat and stroked their ivory Jesuses.

"No," the crowd answered.

"Are we?" he repeated.

"No!" they shouted louder.

I took the bottom of my black dress to my face to catch the nonstop gush of tears, to dab the redness out of my eyes, to stop the dribble from my nose. My lipstick was gone. *Let yourself cry,* I told myself. Until this writing, I hadn't realized how much this struggle was mine too. What, I wonder, might have happened to my own mother had she had the help of a clinic like this? She might not have been so afraid of her illness. She might not have had to suffer so much or been so desperate to take herself off so soon.

Ours is the work of digging. The spade work of struggle. Turning it over and over. That is what I took from the work of political theorist Robert Michels in my graduate social movements class, though he also points out, "Who says organization, says oligarchy." According to the dictum, workers will always defer to leaders.

This can wreak havoc for those of us trained in the principles of worker democracy. *What? Workers will not always want to lead?* When asked what we should do in the face of this truth, Michels says to just keep digging. Even if power tends to concentrate, it's our job to break it up. It's our job to till for change.

Indeed, who knows what you might find.

The rally and action sent ripples throughout the San Francisco Department of Health when the "Professor" was quoted on the local public radio station.

After the rally, we put up our butcher papers and evaluated our campaign. What worked? What didn't? Next steps. Information request follow-up. And so on.

More clinics called about closure threats. This action led to more actions. New leaders emerged.

What they don't tell you in graduate school is that each campaign joins the organizer in the transformation that results from it. In my experience, there is a subjective alchemy some would label as spiritual in these fights. This alchemy happens when there develops a collective commitment to a higher purpose that people are willing to fight for.

It's why when you have any success as an organizer, you keep going back. When your liberation is tied up with everyone else's, you have as much to gain as to lose.

What they also don't tell you in graduate school is that if you are any good at organizing, you will be run out of town. Run out by your own bosses, union bosses, who, with very few exceptions, like the bosses they purport to fight, don't actually want change.

I've been on the run for most of my career. Now retired, I no longer have to be stifled. Have butcher paper. Will travel.

POSTSCRIPT: At SE Geriatric, the positions got found, but not the troll. And although the troll did belch out the promise of filling the positions, the subsequent maze to hiring that would follow would demonstrate new levels of bureaucratic ineptitude and perverse manipulation. After succeeding in saving two more clinics, one in the Bayview and one on Ocean Avenue, I got transferred out of the city. The city bosses complained to the union bosses and I was gone.

CHAPTER 28

IT STARTS OUT SIMPLE ENOUGH

lack phone receiver pressed between his shoulder and ear, the boss opens his hand to a seat at the table opposite his desk. You bend into the chair and lean over a spoonful of rehydrated lentil soup and microwaved Boca burger chunks while he makes his last call. One of your sheer-to-toe stocking legs is crossed over the other, the tips of your black heels pointing to the door.

You hear him tap out the call on his desk phone. A couple more spoonfuls of softened lentils in your mouth, you look up to see the gold letters on the burgundy book spine of the Antonio Gramsci volume that you lent him. The fake meat chunks feel like real meat in your mouth. The phone tapping has stopped. There is no dial tone.

You look up to see him staring at you; his tongue is hanging out of his mouth over his lower lip. His wide, pasty tongue curves under his black brush of a mustache, and his eyes are focused below your neckline on your black cashmere. You match his eyes, and he pulls his tongue back real fast. You put your plastic spoon down, get up, and leave the room.

My God, you say to yourself, closing the door behind you. *Not again.*

You see the tongue wagger leer at junior staff. You notice that there are hours in the day when both disappear, and you wonder. You see a woman who believes that the tongue wagger is in love with her go through stomach staple surgery to lose gross amounts of weight. You see the stapled stomach in a midriff-baring tank top that exposes folds of stretched-out flesh. You wonder what she is thinking.

You wonder what *you* are thinking. You are thinking what everybody else who this happens to is thinking. *This can't really be happening. Nobody does this anymore . . . do they?*

To be sure, you pull down your feminist theory books. The ones you've been dragging around with you during this period of itinerate labor strike organizing.

Objectification. Gender and racial dominance. Reassured, you confirm that what's happening is not about sex; it's about power. It's never about sex. Titillation makes way to fear.

What better way to assert dominance than to reduce the person—in most cases a woman—to a sexual object? It doesn't occur to you until much later that anything you said or did could be perceived as needing to be reminded of who the boss is. It doesn't matter what you think. It's his perception that creates a problem. He has the power.

The irony is that it's your job to represent people who are ogled, touched, propositioned, and harassed in all the listed ways. It's your business: complaining. And even though your work is about complaining, complaining for you is the kiss of death. Any whiff of a complaint would get you blackballed. You'd get a reputation. "Stay away from her," they'd say. "She's trouble." It's understood: you'll never get a job if you complain. You resolve to do battle, as you always have had to, with one hand tied behind your back.

The only way to fight is to continue to do what you do: get the job done, lead in a way that doesn't draw attention to yourself, and most of all, stay in the game. That, after all, is what they most don't want. They want you out. Or they want you down.

I'D SUCCESSFULLY ENGINEERED A COUNTYWIDE strike, helped stop the closure of a public hospital, and negotiated several difficult contracts when I told the tongue wagger I would not renew my contract. In the post-strike clearing, his abuses got worse; he once bragged about being able to underpay an undocumented woman who was on our staff because she was undocumented.

I'd witnessed staff I'd developed conduct their own hearings, develop campaigns, and mobilize actions. These were Latinas and Filipinas, the rank-and-file leaders who became my staff and who I'd mentored and developed. They were exactly the women I wanted to mentor. After one exasperating encounter with the tongue wagger, one of them reminded me of something.

"You know, you have options," she said. *You don't have to stay here, like we do,* was the implication. *You are free to go. We're grateful for what we've learned, but don't stay here because of us. We'll be okay.*

After eighteen months of leering, sexist put-downs, physical threats, screaming, tirades, and hearing people referred to as "dick wads" and "cunts," it was time for me to move on.

To be verbally attacked and threatened by him in front of the staff brought me back to that slap on my face in Tijuana when I was a girl fresh out of that sandy shower. Yet for a long time I felt like I couldn't leave. I sank deeper in what I imagined was the quicksand that swallowed up my mother in any effort she made to resist. I was reminded that the members of my staff were adults too and that I did not have to take care of them. I learned to walk away when he mounted his abuses, and I stopped engaging in the debates he instigated. That only spurred him on.

"When you detach from dysfunction," I was told by an ally outside the union, "he will emotionally bomb you just to provoke you to get back engaged. You are in a no-win domestic abuse cycle that only you can change." Sure enough, like clockwork, he bombed me by threatening to take back my raise. I successfully beat him back without engaging him and made plans to leave.

In the midst of it all, I attended our biannual international union convention. There I heard a speech that reduced me to tears. The speaker, a new officer of the international union, spoke about the abuses he'd suffered as a young Black man. He talked about his mother's fight for dignity after having been fired time after time for refusing to be cowed by an abusive employer. How they'd had to live on fish broth and bread when she had no work.

I sat a seat away from the tongue wagger and leapt from my chair with applause when the speaker finished, tears streaming down my face. That speech helped me see that there was something bigger and more powerful to hold on to.

Following the convention, I continued to do my job, meeting turnout objectives, organizing campaigns, and supporting the staff the best way I could. At the end of one particular meeting with the tongue wagger where we discussed a direct-action street theatre event I'd planned, he commented favorably on the work. I thanked him and then calmly and matter-of-factly told him that I would not be threatened or screamed at by him.

He got up, slammed the conference room door shut behind him so hard that it slammed back open, stormed down the hall to his office, locked himself in, and pulled down the blinds. I didn't see him for the rest of the day.

He learned I was leaving after I'd arranged a series of interviews with other unions. My applications had gotten plenty of interest, and he was still trying to get me to stay. He offered to renew my contract by extending it to begin at the moment of signing as opposed to when it had expired, six months earlier, thereby making it longer. He had his organizing director hack into my computer so he could see where I was applying.

When nothing worked, he said, "I can't get you on work performance, but I'll find something."

On one of my final days there, I sat in the county supervisors' hearing room. A vote had just been taken to grant the beleaguered public hospital one more reprieve. With that done, the strike settled and contracts finished, I got ready to move on, job or no job. I put my copy of Antonio Gramsci into a milk crate next to my books on Chicana feminism.

He came by my office to offer me a letter of recommendation. "Who should I send it to?" he wanted to know. "Make it generic," I said. "That way I can use it as I see fit."

I believed we'd reached some kind of unspoken accommodation. I wouldn't sue him, and he wouldn't trash me. He continued to try everything he could to get me to stay. He even tried to prematurely adjourn an executive board meeting where I'd planned to announce my resignation. I announced it anyway. I never got the letter.

I came to work early on the morning I'd arranged an interview with a union ninety miles away. My background check and the pre-interview went well. I'd spoken with the prospective union's HR person, and she had the papers ready for me to sign. I just needed to meet the union president. They were ready to hire me, she said, but their rules required that he personally make the offer.

I left the office with enough time to avoid being late. I was almost there when they called me to say that something had come up and that they would have to reschedule. "I think I'll only be five minutes late," I said. It's not, that they told me. "Something has happened, we're not sure what." Not letting them finish their sentence, I said, "I'll be there," and hung up the phone. I got there and was told, "We're sorry, they said that you had to come so far, but we still can't arrange a meeting."

I drove back to the office and walked through the kitchen to the conference room where the tongue wagger was holding a staff meeting.

"Got a job?" he said, the sneer dripping down his mouth.

"No," I said. "Thanks for your help."

One by one, every prospect I lined up got knocked down. With all my prospects blocked, I finally took a part-time job to organize a strike at a local university. My boss at the university job helped me get a full-time job. "The word on you is that you are political," the woman who finally hired me into a full-time position told me.

That is what the tongue wagger had managed to contrive. What could I tell her? *No, that's not true. He's sexually harassing me, undermining me with the staff by not giving me full credentials for the convention so that I had to ask a junior staff member for her credentials to go to the bathroom, spreading rumors that I was sleeping with other people at the convention hotel, calling me on a Sunday afternoon, breathing heavily into the phone and clearly jerking off. I'm not suing him because I know that any chance I had to be considered for another job would be dead.*

I got the job, but only on a temporary basis. I also subsequently learned that the tongue wagger had told other prospective employers that I was a coup plotter. That I had tried to turn his staff against him. It was one of the clearest confirmations I've ever had that this whole contest was about power.

My earliest professional experience with sexual harassment occurred when I left my job as a poverty law legal worker to take a job as a union organizer. It was a burnt orange, fall Northwest day just before the heavy rains. The kind of autumn where you can't help but love pumpkins, apples, and scary surprises for your children.

I'd joined in on a legal argument that was taking place in a packed staff meeting. The chief of staff was there with the rest of the staff, and so was his would-be lieutenant, an economist.

"What kind of remedy can we ask for in this kind of case?" the chief of staff wanted to know. The glasses on his face were the kind only newspaper guys of a certain era wore—square, black, and, well, square.

"Can we ask for damages?" he asked.

"No," I said.

"Yes, we can," the economist said.

"Not unless it's built in as an administrative remedy, which isn't likely," I replied.

"So we have to sue them another way?" the chief of staff asked.

"Yes, civilly," I said. "We'll have to sue them in civil court, but I'm not sure we would have standing."

"I still think we can get damages," the economist said, staring at me now, as if saying, *Shut up.*

"We can amend our current complaint," the economist said.

"Okay," the chief of staff said to the would-be lieutenant. "Call the firm and have them send me a memo." He put his glasses back on his head and nodded to me. "And copy her on it."

I dunked the raisin-studded middle of the cinnamon roll in my coffee and sucked it down as we bundled out of the meeting to our offices. The lieutenant walked by me once, close but not too close, his blue against my tweed. He walked by again, this time to get the calculator he'd forgotten. On the way back, he went out of his way to pass me at the coat rack.

Just as he passed me, he pinched my left nipple. He did it so fast I couldn't believe what just happened. I stood there. *Did that asshole just pinch my breast?* I saw him look at me, and I knew that he knew I knew he did it. The look on his face made sure of it.

He had to be sure that I knew. It's the perpetrator's reward, my embarrassment and humiliation. I was so overwhelmed that it felt like I was standing outside myself. That another woman had just been pinched. And I felt like my breast and nipple were the size of a Goodyear Blimp. Bobbing out there in the universe, bumping into everything in sight. All I wanted to do was move away and cover myself up.

I have always regretted that I was so quick to abandon myself. That I didn't have the tools to hold my own vulnerability and to grieve for the young woman who was so despicably attacked. I can see now that, in part, the work I have done all these years has been to stand up for others in a way that I did not have the courage to stand up for myself. The only thing I could summon at the time was contempt with the confirmation that I got to him bad enough to warrant a below-the-belt sucker punch. The message was clear: *You do that again and I will demean you sexually.* I left that organization for other reasons and didn't complain about what he had done to me. I did what lots of us do. I internalized it. If I didn't admit it, it didn't happen. If it didn't happen, I wouldn't have to deal with it, or so I thought. I continued to do my job and learned new ways to fight, contorted though it was, with one hand up in a fist and the other hand tied behind my back.

I got another job with a rival union. Things went well in the new job, well enough for me to be transferred to the Portland office to take on a bigger assignment.

The Portland staff held informal case meetings that anyone could attend, where we discussed various strategies to deal with the employers we organized against. The office dinosaur rarely joined us; he was content to listen from behind his desk with his office door open, his scaly, slimy tail rolled around the doorway.

One day, he decided to join our table. Two of my three colleagues got up and left. Trained in a method of case discussion that welcomed discourse, I was interested in what kind of a case he would bring.

His mixed-and-matched Polo shirt, sweater, and trousers were in the autumn colors his wife had laid out for him. His clothes mocked his Rodan persona. He was central casting for George Meany–era reactionary labor thugs, the type who considered process-oriented public sector union organizers like myself to be social workers. Being called a social worker was a derogatory word for public sector union reps like myself, who in the minds of building trades reps were too afraid to swing a bat when necessary.

"What if you have a guy, a jail janitor, who every time you turn around is crying harassment," he said.

"Is that a statement or a question?" I asked.

"All the boss wants to do is change his shift," he replied.

"So what's the question?" I asked.

"The contract isn't clear about shift changes. So the boss can change him, right?" he said.

"Depends," I replied. "Is there a pattern? Is he the only one that this is happening to? What other rules apply?"

"Hold on, hold on," he said. "The guy is just a janitor who sweeps out cells and cleans up inmate shit."

"So?" I said, smelling a dump truck. "Have you even read his file?" To "dump-truck" a case is to fail to fully investigate it, to find a way to get rid of it while making it look like it was given full consideration and advocacy. Cases like this one, for a Black member, were usually dump-trucked by old-school white male building trades reps. The kind of cases process-oriented "social worker" reps with legal training, like me, would take and fight to the bitter end.

His embroidered Polo pony moved up the left side of his chest as he stretched his arms over his head and pushed out his feet. "Yeah, I read it. It says he's on graveyard because he likes to pinch women's tits."

"I'll bet it does." I leaned into him, crossing my arms over my chest.

His arms down now, he stretched over the table and picked up a blank sheet of paper that was lying there and held it like he was prepared to read from it. He looked up over his glasses and stared at my arms as if he was trying to see through them to my breasts. "Here, I'll read it for you," he said.

"Stop right there," I said, staring right back at him. "I'm putting you on notice. Your conduct is offensive."

He folded his Polo pony behind his arms, then added, "He likes to do other stuff too," like he was about to include new, fictional sexist inventions. He leaned back over the table and brought the piece of paper back up to his sight.

"You've been warned. If you continue, your conduct will constitute harassment," I said.

"Goddamn it to hell," he replied.

"Now you are swearing," I said calmly. I took another sheet of paper and made notes, looked at my watch, and noted the time.

He grabbed his blank sheet of paper, wadded it up, and threw it down. He pushed up from the table, almost knocking the chair over, lumbered back to his office, and slammed the door shut.

My remaining colleague and I just sat and stared at each other. Later that day, I asked my colleague if he would be willing to be a witness to what had just happened. To his credit, he said he would. Frank Vehafric did the right thing.

What followed was months of terror. My office was trashed. My files rifled. He got my secretary to give him copies of all my correspondence. Sudden and loud crashes occurred outside my door. Midnight phone calls. My car was scratched.

I informally went to the bosses. The bosses did nothing. "We know he's an asshole," they said. "He's just an asshole to everybody. It's nothing personal."

When the dinosaur couldn't use me to justify dump-trucking a Black man's case, he had to demean me. It was a new twist on harassment, sexual and racial. The issue was the same, a contest for power.

The harassment only stopped when there was a regime change at the union and the dinosaur was reassigned to our equivalent to Siberia: The Dalles, Oregon.

San Francisco:

One of my many stops during this period of strike organizing was to take a job in San Francisco.

I had just successfully organized testimony to stop the closure of yet another public hospital. The testimony complete, my new boss, a candidate for comb-over counseling, and I sat in the ornate and beautifully sculpted public hearing room at city hall.

Following videotaped and in-person testimony by hospital residents, the appropriate public condemnation was delivered by the necessary complement of sitting elected officials. I knew we'd hit the mark when the politicians went out of their way to condemn any threat of closing the hospital. And when the local business journal days later denounced the testimony, the victory was confirmed.

I sat in the splendor of the hearing room in awe of the residents' courage. They'd come to the hearing in wheelchairs and by special ambulance and at great personal discomfort from their hospital beds to speak to the powerful about their fear of being put out on the street so that liberals could feel good about "deinstitutionalization."

The shimmering chandeliers, sculpted wood, and marble staircases of the ornate hearing room where the powerful deliberated the residents' fate stood in stark contrast with the urine-stained stairwells, paint-chipped turrets, dirty windows, antiquated equipment, and staffing shortages at the turn-of-the-century fortress hospital that was the residents' home.

My boss's boss had been at the hearing and had personally acknowledged the work we'd accomplished before taking her leave from the hearing. Before leaving, she'd handed me her handwritten notes. I held her notes in my lap to review them to see if we needed to add more to the hearing record.

My immediate boss sat next to me in the wooden pews in the middle of the hearing room. We sat on either side of a sculpted armrest. Our boss's notes in my lap, I couldn't help but notice that the hair on his fingers was moving along the wooden grooves of the armrest. It looked like he was rubbing it. I looked back at the notes on my lap.

Through the side of my eyes, I could see that he was manipulating the curves of the wood, rubbing the wood harder and harder as if to sexually stimulate it. I looked up at him and he was staring at me with his tongue against his cheek, his eyes on my breasts. I got up and moved across the aisle.

Here it was again, demeaning sexual objectification in response to a successful demonstration of power.

I had been hired in a temporary position at this union and therefore had no job protection; if offered a permanent assignment, I would have to go through a lengthy probation. The armrest rubber knew that.

On another occasion, the armrest rubber planted his feet squarely on top of mine under a conference table where I was leading an arbitration preparation meeting for a junior colleague. I felt something on top of my feet, not sure if something this weird could be happening, his feet on top of mine under the conference table on the eleventh floor of a building near downtown San Francisco.

Committed to finishing my argument, feet or no feet, I carried on. He stared right at me and dug his feet in. I stared back. I knew he knew. He had to be sure I did. Just like with the tongue wagger, I continued what I was doing, prepared to go on to finish the job.

Later, when I had time to think about what had happened, it occurred to me that this had taken some forethought on the foot masher's part. *When she sits down, I will put my feet on top of hers. That'll shut her up.*

How practiced too. If caught, an easy retreat. "Oh, I'm so sorry, I didn't know those were your feet." The symbolism of being underfoot was unmistakable.

What became obvious in my dealings with the armrest-rubber-cum-foot-masher was his limited skill at the bargaining table.

And even though I had bargained hundreds of contracts, the only position I was offered at the bargaining table was as his secretary. I declined his offer.

I witnessed him discount and disrespect the testimony of his own members (women mostly) as they told management about what they faced in maternity wards in public hospitals. When the nurses spoke about the near-death babies they held, the needlestick injuries they suffered, fighting for bedside time with immigrant, non-English-speaking women, I felt a fullness in my chest as I sat with them. It united me to them and all vulnerable women at that moment of death and birth as well as the women who were there to help them give birth far away from their homes in a country where they did not speak or understand the language or culture.

It was hard to hear their eloquent and passionate testimony slapped shut because the armrest rubber didn't know how to manage the power of it. Instead, he appeared to be more worried about protecting his relationship with the hospital's management representative.

As time went on, I'd learned to expect "inadvertent" elbows at my breast, armrest-rubber stares, exclusions from critical meetings, accusations that I was trying to undermine him, an attempt to remove me from the premises, and finally a contrived complaint against me.

For the first time in all the years that I had done this work, I decided to formally complain when the armrest-rubber-cum-foot-masher attempted to use a complaint he'd contrived to issue a disciplinary action against me. He convinced a member leader to get a member to lie about something I did or didn't do and put it in the form of a member complaint. At this point, in my over twenty-five years of professional work, I had never had a complaint filed against me. He was determined to discredit me when, I learned later, he became afraid that I would take his job during a union restructuring. I had no interest or intention of doing so, but like the situation with the tongue wagger, I learned that it was his fear and distorted perception that created the problem.

This time I complained because my reputation was at stake.

Complaining isn't easy, even for union organizers. The process itself is simple enough, but the psychological cost is immense. My office had no natural light. It was like a cave lit only by fixtures I placed around it to avoid overhead fluorescent lighting. On one side of my laptop I had the language of the union's anti-harassment policy and the state law prohibiting sexual harassment. The words wended down a single letter at a time. Alone, one by one, the tap-tap of the words sounded loud, like they were taking over the small room. Even though I'd typed these phrases many times on behalf of members, I had to type my own one stretch of time at a time, each time reviewing the drafts, sometimes by minutes, hours, days, or just seconds at a time. Like laying down track, each step I took made way for the next.

Along the way, I had to make peace with myself, and I had to reach back to everything I had internalized. I had nightmares and flashbacks and became depressed. Through it all, I had to forgive myself and I had to be willing to forgive the perpetrator. It didn't mean I actually needed to forgive him; it just meant I needed to be willing to. It was the only way I could get free. I also learned that forgiveness does not have to be cheap. It could and would take its time.

Slowly, I let go of any attachment to grandiose victories, and I learned to be grateful for simple but meaningful everyday redemptions. As the path became clearer, I knew that I wanted nothing more than to stand up for my good name.

When I finally complained, I complained not because sexual harassment policies existed—policies have always existed—but because after the union's merger, women had come into increasing power, and I had developed relationships with many of them who knew and respected my work. I had learned to trust them.

Even so, I sought the help of a law firm to advise me about the best strategy to employ.

"Be prepared," the lawyer said. "Once you raise this in any formal way, you risk being labeled as a capital-C complainer," he emphasized. I had to weigh this ignominy against the further trashing of my reputation by my old boss with a new boss.

I took a trusted male colleague with me to the meeting with the union's new chief of staff. My colleague was a man who'd earned his movement stripes through anti-apartheid work in South Africa. He stood by me even though he and I were both on probation at the time. I will always remember his courage and support. I will always be grateful to David Canham.

The day of the complaint, my colleague and I walked into a room that had been named for a deceased member leader whom I'd met twenty years before, when I'd come to California from Oregon as a new union organizer to an international union convention. This member leader and I had organized the first-ever women of color caucus at that convention. What sweet symmetry, I thought, to be in Lorraine's room. I felt like I was being true to what we'd set out to do all those years before and that she was there in the room with me.

And I will always be grateful for the chief of staff who heard my complaint. She responded quickly and arranged for us to meet at the earliest possible time. She made eye contact, listened, and assured me that my complaint would be taken seriously.

My notes in hand, I outlined in two hours what had happened to me over two years. Part of the difficulty was that I had to protect the institution I loved and the work I had dedicated my life to at the same time that I had to protect myself from it.

My steps, though cautious and tentative at first, had the desired effect. The perpetrator was exposed, and I was given another assignment. Even after the complaint was filed, he continued to stand too close to me, the last time right behind me, directing angry, hateful glares my way. It didn't matter that the chief of staff who heard the complaint was in the room. It was as sneaky and creepy as when we were in city hall and it was clearly about power; it was as much about forcing his will on me as it was about undermining her.

No matter how many years of therapy I've had or self-help groups I've attended, strikes I've led, or bosses I've fought, I know I will miss some, if not most, of what comes at me. It's so pervasive, it's a given that I will. So I've learned to go in forgiving myself, recognizing that I won't get it all. That some of it will get by me. Or even get me.

It's okay. I will fight the ones I see. And, with help, we will win some too.

CHAPTER 29

AIN'T DOIN' IT

In the late '90s, the union I worked for held its biannual convention in Pendleton, Oregon. With time to kill, some of us took Pendleton's Underground City Tour. A nineteenth-century eastern Oregon railroad stop, Pendleton, like the rest of the state, had had racist sundown laws since the 1850s. Chinese workers who had followed the railroad stayed and did service work for the town when the railroad work ended. After sundown, they could be shot if found on the street, so they built a city under the city. Glass pavement blocks provided needed light. There were laundries, a bathhouse, boot-cleaning services, herbal dispensaries, a jail, opium dens, and more. You could get a bath for ten cents. The next bath in the same water would be eight cents, and so on, until the water was too filthy to bathe in. Near the exit of the tour, the Chinese government had dedicated a gong to honor the memory of its many citizens who had suffered and died in this city under a city.

The rest of the tour took us to the top of the city, where women kept in "cribs" worked in the upstairs brothels. There were hidden doors leading to escape hatches that went down winding back-alley stairways, card tables that could instantly become tea tables, brass beds with nineteenth-century corsets and lady-of-the-evening attire draped over them. On Sunday mornings, the parlor was turned over to the parson, who conducted special services for women too tainted by the brothel trade to attend regular Sunday services.

The union hired a local country-western band for the convention's Saturday night dance. The musicians were outfitted in the requisite belt buckles, cowboy boots and hats, and pearl-snap shirts with fringe and floral decorations. The singers looked like the cowboy singers my Utah grandma used to love to watch when I was a kid.

We all got up and did some line dancing and some square dancing. Having spent part of my childhood in Utah, I could keep up with the major turns and steps.

The floor show continued as we sat down to another pitcher of beer, culminating in a simulated lynching, complete with a noose and rope. The veil of separation between the band and me had been not only pierced but shredded. I saw the twisted face of the band member who held the noose around his neck. Everyone at my table, including me, turned to see the noose and then turned right back to the table like nothing had happened.

That memory, like so many in Oregon, became a part of a moving landscape I instinctively wrapped in denial, a skill I'd learned as a child in Utah. This was the not-so-hidden racist Oregon of the 1990s, mimicking its not-so-hidden racist past. In 1887, just more than a hundred years earlier, thirty-one Chinese miners were massacred in Hells Canyon, Oregon, by seven white horse thieves. When one of the killers came forward and named the other perpetrators, a white jury failed to convict them. A Chinese life was not worth a white life.

My path to becoming the chief spokesperson for the District Council of Trade Unions (DCTU), a coalition of city and building trade unions that bargained together for a contract with the city of Portland, was not a straight shot. The only woman of color in its history to hold that title, I had to fight for it. Even though I had seniority, my boss hired a white guy from outside the union to bargain the contact. He was a drunk. When his misrepresentations got too bad, it was clear he had to go. I dropped my pending grievance against the boss when he agreed to give me the job, but I was definitely not his first choice.

My contract campaign style, in contrast with that of most reps, was bottom up. I spent little time getting to know the bosses or building relationships with them but rather worked with and built a base among the members whose contracts I was negotiating. Meeting the boss was for later and only if necessary, and even then it was always in the company of members. Spending time with mid-level city bosses was not a good use of my energy. I would meet who I needed to meet as the campaign went on, but the members came first. It was they who had the power to make any necessary changes in their working conditions. And I needed to know who could or would fight if it got down to that.

I went to a regularly scheduled noontime membership meeting held in the maintenance yard's lunchroom. Lunch buckets like the ones my stepdad carried to the railroad yard clicked open. It felt comfortable, familiar. I could drop the armor I got used to wearing in the elite spaces I'd learned to navigate when I left my neighborhood and made it through college to do "professional" work. Landing there was like I'd stolen fire from the gods and was there to bring it back home.

The room was full; the guys—mostly guys and mostly white—were all there to check out the new rep. I moved away from the stand-in-the-front-of-the-room lecture format of question taking. Instead, I chose a round table setting, to the extent we could manage it with lunch benches, and had a sheet of paper on the wall for notes, if needed.

Questions came from all over the room. Contracts in hand, they questioned my knowledge and my position on outstanding issues, and raised new issues. The elected chapter officers were nowhere to be found—which was unusual, as they would generally ceremonially welcome the new rep. This would, it appeared, not be a courtesy extended to me. I had to do the meeting cold. By the looks of it, they'd decided to throw me to the wolves to see what would happen. I was glad they weren't there—that way I didn't have to dance on ceremony for them either, by according them respect without knowing much about them but their titles.

After the chapter's previous contract was ratified, the members found out that their ironclad, state-of-the-art anti-contracting-out language had been weakened in the contract. They turned on the rep, who was blamed and transferred to a small coastal town. Through my research, I learned that it was my boss who had opened the door on the contracting-out change. Until then, the language had been the tightest I'd ever seen in a contract. Now I knew why the other big unit reps didn't want the boss at their tables.

As the meeting took shape, a cadre of questioners emerged. Ed Smith led the crew. He wanted to know what the union was going to do about a particular long-standing violation, an issue that the president and the previous rep had ignored. The issues went up on the wall.

I was trained in the "organize first, grieve later" school of labor organizing. I had legal training, but time after time I'd learned that direct action was more effective than filing grievances. Members trained in direct-action methods exercised agency and were empowered to make changes that made them less dependent on reps and quasi-legal grievance systems that took the issues off the shop floor.

As the meeting wound down, I told all assembled that the following week—same time, same place—I would be there to conduct a work session to deal with the issues they had raised. Anyone was welcome, but whoever showed up had to be ready to work. Sure enough, the group that showed up was a smaller one, and the loudest complainers were nowhere to be found. Again, the union officers did not attend, but Ed Smith was there with his crew.

Using a problem-solving method I developed to meet the constraints of an hour-long lunch break, we listed, prioritized, and came up with a battle plan for a particular outstanding issue. We also made a commitment to meet every week to report back, measure progress, and adjust as needed. Using simple escalation tactics like group breaks, slogan stickers, and petitions, we started to deal with issues that mattered to the members.

As we started to make some headway, more members joined our efforts. They provided new insight to the issues and, most important, brought with them a treasure trove of information we could not otherwise have gotten. They knew the bosses' pressure points better than I did and were able to be strategic about where and when to push.

Using an *Art of War*–inspired approach to engagement that I'd learned in graduate school, I realized that small, direct hits went a long way, left open a vast array of responses for either side to make, and, most of all, minimized risk if a group performed them.

It didn't take long for my boss to call me into his office to talk to me about concerns the chapter's elected president had brought to him. The president had complained about the organizing we were doing, saying he felt excluded and not consulted about our campaigns. This was code for his inability to "get things done" with his middle-management contacts, who had stopped relying on him to broker issues.

I told the boss everyone was invited to our weekly strategy meetings, including the president and his officers. He was free to participate, but he had chosen not to; furthermore, he did not now have the right to veto any action taken by the newly formed direct-action team.

The clincher was that the president's girlfriend was on staff in the political department of the union and wanted to be part of any meeting we held with elected city council officials. They had also started to take notice of the issues we were working on and solving.

The Portland system at the time was a portfolio system. City bureaus—water, planning, police, etc.—were assigned to elected city council members by the mayor. Once assigned, the bureaus were under the purview of their respective elected officials. This meant that as we continued to build power, members could get things done directly with their elected bosses. With their new tools, members could hurt or help a politician, and they knew it. They didn't need a broker.

I consulted with the members about bringing the president's girlfriend into the campaigns, and they wanted nothing to do with her. The president, they said, could participate like everyone else did and was invited to show some leadership.

The monthly membership meetings got bigger as more issues got addressed and more bureaus—planning, fire, and transportation—started their own organizing committees and campaigns. Contract negotiations with the city were imminent, as were chapter elections. The new base of leaders decided to run on a slate against the incumbents.

I didn't involve myself in who would run in the member elections and who wouldn't. My only job was to see to it that the elections were free and fair, and that the election process adhered to any applicable state and federal laws.

The new slate consisted of leaders from different departments where we had active campaigns. The campaigns we ran brought in new, tested leaders. If we were going to be a force against what we knew was coming—more city take-backs in contracting out, and the city's insolvent, self-run health plan, which was bleeding money every day—we had to know who could fight and fight to win.

The incumbent president campaigned on the second shift at the police department under the influence of alcohol. Word spread and he was toast.

Lunch-bucket, Wonder bread sandwich–eating, work-yard activist Ed Smith handily won the presidency. We had new leaders from Planning and Police as well. A coiled python with the words "Ready to Strike" was the new slate's motto.

One key chink in the works was one of the union's executive board members, a person whom my boss answered to. She was also the treasurer of the city chapter. She didn't like that we were spending chapter money on the campaigns, and didn't understand or support organizing.

Like in a video game, the stronger the chapter got, the bigger its foes became, both inside and outside the union. And it wasn't just city middle managers or out-of-touch leaders—we now faced the union's institutions, along with the city's.

My boss supported the big rallies we organized and made the necessary appearances, because doing those things made him look good. Our largest kickoff rally was in January, to honor Dr. Martin Luther King. King was in Memphis to support striking sanitation workers affiliated with the city chapter's national union when he was shot and killed at the Lorraine Motel. We brought forth his memory as an advocate of workers and marched for justice in his name. For our mostly white members, this was personal.

This labor rally to honor Dr. King was a first in many respects, and probably the first ever in Oregon, especially in light of Oregon's racist history. A legacy of Oregon's sundown laws was a mostly white state. The sundown laws targeted anyone nonwhite, specifically African Americans. There were so few Black people in Oregon when the Klan was in power there in the 1920s, its targets were Catholics. The longshore union had a long history of racist hiring practices at the Oregon docks.

As city chapter power grew, behind the scenes my boss was working with some chapter leaders to break up the city's team and undermine my leadership at the table. One chapter leader, a white guy from Police who did his bidding, ultimately got a job with the union.

As we drew closer to a strike, we organized rallies and my boss would order me to a different meeting so he and the president's girlfriend could head the rallies. But by then it didn't really matter, because the members had been trained in direct-action methods and had successfully carried them out. We'd built a solid, ground-up campaign that included prime-time aerial visuals of city hall surrounded by umbrellas. "Rain or shine, ready to strike," was one slogan. When we got bogged down by procedural roadblocks, we literally wrapped city hall in red tape to make the point. Cameras followed us as we pulled red tape around the building's marble ballasts.

It was getting clearer that whatever he did, my boss couldn't co-opt or control me like he had with the previous rep, who was blamed for the language changes the boss made and got transferred to the coast.

The union's city parking deputies decided to issue warnings instead of tickets one day throughout the city. They had always maintained the discretion to issue warnings or tickets in any particular situation. The warning tickets were red; the tickets were white. This effort coincided with citywide union members wearing red to demonstrate their anger about the city's well-publicized plan to cut their health care benefits. Red warnings stacked up on windshields outside large downtown department stores where people parked all day. Revenue losses due to lack of car turnover were huge. Now downtown businesses, the mayor's base, were starting to feel the pain.

There were two things I carried with me to every meeting I attended: a calendar of legal deadlines leading up to a strike date based on Oregon public-employee law, and a map that showed where concentrations of members were. We used both to strategically plan our campaign. At any given time, everybody knew where we were and where we were going, and that could change as new opportunities emerged.

In previous contract fights, contract expirations came and went, with no effective leverage to close an agreement before it expired. It was not unusual for members to work without a contract for months or even years. The members' escalating actions made the strike threat real to the city and to themselves.

As part of their strike plan, the members undertook a bureau-by-bureau departmental research campaign to uncover city waste and questionable spending and began to expose it. We had the city's budget analyzed by the union's DC economists and discovered that the city indeed had plenty of discretionary income, notwithstanding the mayor's claims about funds earmarked for her pet projects.

We also learned that unless structural changes took place, there was not enough discretionary money to offset the losses incurred by a mishandled, nearly insolvent, self-managed health plan—especially one that was subject to exorbitant rate hikes by providers.

To publicly expose the city's questionable spending, we organized a tour of "Porkland." We hired a bus and loaded it with union members, like Ken Kesey's merry pranksters, to tour the city of Portland and expose where the city spent money on "pork." One such offense was the mayor's well-known backdoor deals with the baseball stadium owners.

Using street theater like California's Teatro Campesino, I wrote a script for a skit to illustrate how big money between the mayor and big business changed hands. The skit, the rally, and pigs on ropes, brought in by our members in front of the ballpark, got prime-time coverage. Next, the tour of Porkland went to the trolley station, where the city spent loads of money on trolleys to ferry its well-heeled from one elite destination to another in an area of town that was being developed as the Pearl District, now home to million-dollar properties. Finally, our tour culminated at the esplanade, a pathway that cost thousands of dollars and that would later serve as a monument to the mayor.

Our slogan was "An inch of the planned esplanade will cover health costs for a worker's family."

The city claimed that these funds were restricted earmarks but had little of substance to say about the pockets of discretionary money we found in its budget; it also refused to respond to suggested cost savings our members found in their respective bureaus.

We got noon and prime-time coverage for the tour of Porkland campaign. The union's political department complained that we were making the city look bad by exposing all its pork and that average citizens would not understand.

I continued to move the table forward, rejecting the city's take-backs. My boss continued to try to pick off my team and even made inroads with the rest of the reps who represented the DCTU, including machinists, laborers, plumbers, electricians, and others.

In one instance, a member of the electrical workers was so unnerved by the grief our public campaign was causing the mayor and the city that he threatened to go to the city and tell them our bottom line.

One day I came to the table and was set upon by the DCTU reps. I sat and listened amid direct attacks, threats, and open challenges.

"Okay," I said. "Here." I closed the bargaining book, removed myself from the chair, stepped away, and invited each one of them individually to take the chair. One by one, they slumped over in their seats.

"Go ahead," I urged them, "take the chair, I will support you one hundred percent. What, none of you? Okay then, let's get back to work, and I don't want to hear any more bullshit."

That's when my boss decided to join the table—at whose urging, who knows?

"Just give them something on contracting out," he said to me privately.

"What?" I looked straight at him. "I'm not giving them shit. We're already going to take a hit on health care. They don't get job security too. Ain't doin' it."

As our campaigns progressed, all of our bargaining sessions were now at city hall. While others in the chapter, under heavy influence from my boss, started to peel away, Ed Smith and his crew never wavered. They had by far the biggest base. They were solid. They knew their contract, and they knew its history of sideways take-backs. Nobody was going to put anything past them.

The city kept watered-down contracting-out language and huge health care take-backs on the table. We kept fully paid medical coverage on the table, even when it became clear from our own audits and economists that the system would soon be insolvent without member contributions. Not only was the plan mismanaged, but local health plans like these were also victims of the national hemorrhage caused by health care corporations who had been bleeding the country by jacking up rates in the late '90s. The era of fully paid medical insurance was over for most American workers.

If we couldn't stop it entirely, the obvious move was to build in a percentage on the salary base and link it to a health care index, COLA, that would grow with the structural base of salaries to offset any health insurance increases and to cap premiums, out-of-pocket costs, and co-pays. The best we could do at the table was to put together a package that would blunt the impact of it.

Our members would eventually decide what they were willing to take or strike for. But a deal that weakened job security was a nonstarter as far as I was concerned. As obscure as the change could look at the moment, affecting only a limited number of members in the DCTU, mostly in nonprofessional classifications, its potential long-term effect was ominous. Over time, the city could wipe out most represented jobs, especially in the unskilled trades, and our members knew it.

As we continued our campaign against the city, the firefighters joined in and made picket signs for us. They knew they were next. The president of the police union joined us at an action at the North Portland police precinct. The city had proposed closing the community precinct, and we organized with the community to try to stop the closure. Our direct-action campaign involved chalk-outlined bodies at the doorsteps of the soon-to-be-closed precinct.

A procession of carnations were laid on the chalk corpses by our members and community participants to illustrate bodies of the dead in the underserved Black and Brown working-class neighborhood. As with many of our direct-action campaigns, it made for a great visual and the cameras loved it.

The community again questioned the mayor's priorities. Would she be so quick to pull resources away from more well-heeled neighborhoods, trolleys for the downtown elite, questionable deals with stadium owners, and an esplanade with her name on it? Our campaigns always included some element of community impact.

As we got closer to our strike date, it was time to take what we had to our members and let them decide what they would accept. None of our team wanted to lose ground on health care costs. Even as we were able to cauterize the hit and offset actual costs by adding a percentage onto the salary base to get us through the next contract, it was not popular and our member leaders at the bargaining table would not recommend it.

The city and union hacked away at it, session after session. In our closed caucus, when we had a final proposal, I became the focus of our members' rage. It was one of the hardest meetings I ever attended, fomented in part by my boss's behind-the-scenes machinations with some of the leaders. When the rage and venting, much of it directed at me, happened, my boss stepped out of the way and let me take the brunt of it. He just sat there, doing nothing to redirect it or address the issues we faced in the fight.

When everybody left, a member who had quietly followed the campaign came to sit beside me. She took my hand in hers and said, "You have been generating a lot of legitimate rage at the city about what is happening to all of us. Now you have to stand in front of it for us to move forward. It's not about you." We both wept.

Despite my boss's insistence, we gave no ground on contracting out. We took what we had to our members. They overwhelmingly voted it down. They were ready to strike. The day was set, and the proper notices were filed. Our members would strike before they gave in on health care. That much was clear.

I was at the gym, where it was quiet and I could think, for my daily early-morning workout when I saw television footage of the Twin Towers bursting into flames. It kept repeating in a loop. I made it to the office and turned on the TV in the lunch-room. The mayor and police chief called a press conference to try to assure Portland that they were doing everything possible to keep the city safe. There was open speculation that cities on the East and West Coasts could be the next targets. The mayor suggested that people tape plastic in their windows.

A strike was looming. Picket signs had been distributed, and picket captains had their orders. We had a bargaining session scheduled for the last day of the contract. I'd learned that my boss had tried and failed to get a photo op with the mayor to make assurances about public safety. As we got closer to the midnight strike deadline, picket signs in hand, our members organized rallies at their respective buildings.

Once the last offer was voted down, everything was back on the table, including the contracting-out language we had fought so hard to keep out. A state mediator was called in. My boss ordered me to sit right next to him.

The mediator suggested that members be separated from the table. Without consulting the team, my boss agreed. The members had to watch through a glass door. The mayor and the heretofore-absent HR director joined the session. The mayor's immediate demand was that I make an apology. I just sat there and stared straight at her and said nothing.

It was getting closer to midnight. I then witnessed something I will never forget and that saddens me to this day. My boss started to plead with the mayor to take the union's last proposal.

"Don't ask me," the mayor responded. "Ask her." She pointed at the city's HR director. My boss winced but continued his plea to the HR director. Did he wince because the mayor deflected him to a subordinate for his pleading, or because the HR director was an out Black woman, or both?

That's where the world stopped for me. The code in my 'hood was that you never pleaded. If you were going to get your ass whipped, you took it. You didn't beg.

Worse, a baseline labor principle is that you never, ever make any agreement with the boss without the members present. The bargaining team knew something wasn't right as they watched through the glass window in the door.

The city representatives decided to go into a caucus. It was after midnight. The strike at the police bureau and the sewers had started. My boss sent a directive for them to stand down, pending the city's response, without even knowing what the city's response was.

After what seemed like a very long caucus, the city team came back to the table without the mayor or the HR director. It was now three or four o'clock in the morning. My counterpart on the city's side looked crushed. They would accept our last proposal with small changes on health care to see where we could find further health care savings. All that would be worked out in committee. Word went out that there was a tentative agreement. Details were to follow.

We went back to the table to hammer out final changes. My boss attended one meeting and then backed away, leaving me to finish it. My goal at holding the line on job-security take-backs had been met. The healthcare deal we struck was essentially the first deal we made. Another ratification vote was scheduled, and the proposal was overwhelmingly accepted.

The weekly tabloid that had been covering the campaign featured me on the front page as "the woman who almost shut down Portland." Word got back to me that my boss was furious. He had wanted the spotlight.

When the contract was ratified and I got back to the office, disciplinary action awaited me for some pretext violation related to the parking deputy action. My boss's boss on the union's executive board wanted my hide. In his begging, my boss had forgotten or neglected to get the outstanding unfair-labor-practice charges removed as part of the deal. It was standard for that to happen at the end of any agreement—a sort of clearing of the deck. I would not have been surprised if, through some back channel, he had let it be known that there would be some internal discipline for what the city now described as the wildcat parking deputy illegal strike.

In short order, not only was I under disciplinary action, but my boss cut ties with the union's longtime woman-led law firm that was advising the campaign. It seemed that the executive board member was upset at her too, so my boss rolled on her.

I hired a firm to represent me against the union and was cleared. The union had to pay fines for the so-called wildcat strike. Not long after that, I decided to leave the union. Job offers once made to me were withdrawn. It got back to me that my boss had blackballed me. In subsequent years, the contracting-out language has been changed and one large member of the DCTU left the coalition and bargains on their own against the city.

CHAPTER 30

YOU GOTTA KEEP
THE DEVIL IN THE HOLE

I walked the cliffside path to and from the statue of Santa
Monica and the Hotel Shangri-La, probably right by fugitive
crime boss Whitey Bulger, who had been hiding in Santa
Monica in plain sight.

I was a kid from Salt Lake when we moved to a neighborhood not fifteen miles from there. I stepped with the bob and nod
of young South Central brothers who sported black do-rags and
neatly folded shirts over their forearms and who didn't seem to
notice grade-school Mexican girls. With his white shirt, necktie,
and trim mustache, my second-grade teacher Mr. Washington,
his catcher's mitt hands around my skinny brown wrists, showed
me how to stop a hard, flying tetherball before it hit me.

A glass bead chain down the side of her face, my English
teacher, Mrs. Walker, peered over us.

"No socializing, fraternizing, or talking to yourself."

She taught me to pop open, dissect, and operate with words,
and she didn't suffer cheats.

I was on unemployment after the nurses' union fired me, beached in Venice, California, and sending out résumés. I'd left a twenty-year work history in Portland, Oregon, to take the nurse union job.

On a daily walk, I picked up a rock in the sand. Flat, oval, and warm in my palm, it said, "Hang in there." I put it in my pocket and rubbed it against my thigh.

I didn't have stacks of money stashed in the wall like Whitey did when they caught him, but, living lean, I kept my monthly expenses to below a month of unemployment. I'd learned the hard way not to get comfortable.

Days went by. Another rock.

"Your wanting empowers evil. They don't care! Ask God. Take my fear now!"

An answer to my ruminations about the nurses' union where staff abuse was okay in the name of the revolution. It belied its public image as a union of worker/health-care advocates. Its staff was overworked, spied on, and ordered to undermine and counter-organize elected rank-and-file leaders. I got a midnight call from my boss during a caucus at the bargaining table, urging me to take a settlement that the sketchy mediator wanted. I'd never been called in the middle of closing a deal by a boss at the behest of a mediator. The mediator had tried to get me to sell her my car for her son in a kind of twisted quid pro quo. It all felt like a fix. No car, no deal—I was out. The whole experience was a case of "the bigger the front, the bigger the back."

A friend who'd warned me against the nurses' union brought me a plaster Virgen de Guadalupe, its bright-red-and-teal starry shroud bold against blue-white ocean waves. I gave my friend a plaster Yeshiva boy I'd found in one of the thrift stores I spent my days in while I waited for work, along with the bookstores and libraries where I resumed my study of Shakespeare and the coffee shops where I tried to write and could hear book and movie deals being negotiated. In the mornings I heard the sax-playing skateboarder whiz by, and on Friday nights I had dinner at Mao's Kitchen.

The next message came on a three-sided rock.

Side A: "You are not in balance yet. Your ego is compelled to act, but stop and adapt."

Side B: "Follow your values."

Side C: "Say, 'God, take my fear.'"

My virgin-bearing friend offered me a job at the worker training center she directed. The offer was generous, but I had to decline. I love to train, but at my core I am an organizer.

Last rock: "You're waiting for the renewal, then you're the leader in removing corruption."

At the bottom it said, "Future = Power."

I almost dropped that rock when I read it. The rocks weighing down my gym pants against my thighs, I reached to pet them now and then to soothe myself.

I got a job as the union representative for City of Oakland workers—technically, their authorized legal representative, an agent of their union.

I looked up from my desk to find blue, black, and pink, her hair in a hard black curve around her full brown face, on her lips, the slightest pink. Her heavy, stiff, blue City of Oakland parking deputy uniform broke over the curves of her body and the openness of her heart. I'll call her Parking Deputy Sista.

"I willed you here," she said from my doorway.

Never one to underestimate the power of parking deputies, I sat up right-angle straight. City of Portland parking deputies carried out a series of wildcat strikes throughout the city to protest bad working conditions and health care cuts. All day, cars parked up and down in front of downtown Portland department stores with red warning notices flapping on their windshields instead of tickets. Retail revenue losses were huge.

"I've never been 'willed' anywhere before," I said.

Union organizers are the blessing and the curse of the labor movement. We build worker power to change the relationship between our members and their bosses. New rank-and-file leaders also bring a dynamic dialectic to the institution of the union, agitating against its tendency to concentrate power. Organizing is the only antidote I know to the cronyism and patrimony so endemic to unions, a ramrod to break up what Robert Michels called the "iron law of oligarchy."

After successful community campaigns to stop the closure of San Francisco clinics in the Bayview, in the Mission, and on Ocean Avenue, I was run out or, rather, "relocated" for my "protection," for having reported a harasser, my boss.

Run out of Berkeley for organizing the units under a powerful union executive board member who then tried to get me fired and who said that organizing was "the Devil." Run out of Portland for the wildcat parking-deputy strikes and for front-page weekly tabloid coverage when we shut down the whole city for a few hours. Run out after a successful Monterey County strike and for refusing to sleep with that boss.

Before accepting Oakland, I was offered a job in the union's education department, one with more money, more control of my schedule, minimal oversight, and a leg up to a possible post-retirement teaching gig.

"No, thanks," I said. "I'm grateful, but I need to organize."

After the Portland and Monterey County strikes, Oakland was wide open.

I'd survived the ghetto, my mother's mental illness, my stepfather's alcoholism, and their vicious abuse; fought ignorance, racism, sexism, and classism; and survived cancer, which had given me a gift, a place to locate my innate drive and predisposition. I had the power to make meaningful change in the lives of working people and in my own life.

Organizing meant what my graduate research professor described as "following the dog." He meant it in a research context. I practiced it in an organizing context, following the organizing problem wherever it led.

What kept me going, like the rocks in the sand, were the fierce, loving hearts of working people, who, no matter how dressed up it was, knew bullshit when they saw it.

The City of Oakland union chapter was in transition. The million-plus-member international union it was part of was merging ten unions to one to create a several-thousand-member, multicity, multicounty, public- and private-sector Bay Area union.

"Okay," I said to Parking Deputy Sista. "What do we got?"

"A key steward is in the hole and has been there for weeks," she said.

"The hole?" I asked.

"Yeah, they put her on paid administrative leave pending an investigation. They won't say for what. The city is ordering us to issue only parking warnings up the hill, where the rich white folks live, and parking tickets down the hill, where the Black, Latino, and poor folks live. The revenue department is a mess, and the building inspectors are getting the shaft. The library is ready to decertify the union."

"Okay, okay," I said. "Bring it all to our organizing conference."

Union stewards from major city departments huddled around butcher paper for two days and, using a direct-action campaign method I developed, charted out the broken bones, missing teeth, diseased marrow, and still-beating heart that made up the City of Oakland.

"You mean the city directs you to only give warnings up the hill?" I said. "And tickets in the flatlands?"

"Yes, they do," rang out a chorus of parking deputies in different tones and timbres around the butcher paper.

"You got paper on that?" I asked.

Their hands in the air waved off the question. "Paper, yeah, we got tons of paper. Don't worry about that," they said.

"Paper, meaning memos or other documentation," I clarified.

More waving. "Don't worry, we got it," they insisted.

A deputy flipped to a clean page. "It's like this." He drew a line diagonally across the paper. "Here's 580. Our routes are divided. Up the hill, it's only warnings. Down the hill, it's only tickets. That simple," he said.

"Wow," I replied.

I walked around like I had a gold nugget in my pocket and hoped nobody would try to steal it.

The de facto president of the City of Oakland union chapter tried to end the conference without a commitment to time and resources. One of the stewards pulled out a side table, and I rolled in the master plan and calendar we had created. We settled on Monday meetings after work in the first-floor conference room to launch our citywide campaign, starting with the parking deputies; hence the "Monday Night Crew" was born. I resolved to work with the de facto president one-on-one, ascribing his reticence to inexperience.

Throughout the conference, the de facto president's sidekick, a short, balding white man with big glasses, touched my foot with his and made himself indispensable. I moved away. He moved closer. On it went. Here it was again: fight him off and focus on the larger fight—the double bind.

What I didn't know was that the de facto president had not been elected and that he had a special arrangement whereby he was on "lost time" work release from his job at the City of Oakland Public Works Department. He received full city pay and benefits, reported to no one at the city or at the union, and was left to make unvetted changes to the labor contract.

Pulling strings on the city management side was the union's former staff director, who had been forced out during the merger. She wasn't the first union executive to trade sides to work for the bosses.

Soon enough, a draft agreement that would have materially changed job-security provisions in the labor contract came across my desk for a signature. I sent it back to the city with the corrected language. It kept coming back, and I kept sending it back.

The de facto president and his sidekick denied any knowledge of this draft agreement. One day the absent, unelected vice president showed up looking for the deal they'd made with city management before I got there.

I wrote to the city manager and her boss and sent a copy to the city attorney telling her there would be no changes and demanding that any further correspondence related to the City of Oakland chapter be sent to me. Anything short of that would constitute unfair labor practice (ULP) for "direct dealing" with anyone other than the legally authorized labor representative for the union.

Along with his lost-time work-release agreement, the de facto president got an office at the union, Fridays off, and an assistant, the sidekick. Before long, the City of Oakland chapter operated on two levels. Upstairs, the de facto president and his sidekick were trying to play while getting played by the city. When he tried to negotiate the settlement of an action without consulting the Monday Night Crew, they withheld action details from him. Downstairs, the Monday Night Crew met to carry out their master organizing plan.

The de facto president liked to grandstand at events we mobilized. When the front-page racist ticketing story broke, he told me that union representatives didn't do public speaking and that any quotes for the press would go through him. Cameras descended on the parking deputies at their city hall press conference. We had early morning print, TV, and radio coverage. Outraged members of the public came up from the flatlands with tickets in hand.

Parking Deputy Sista was quoted saying words to the effect of, "We are here to serve, not harm, the people of Oakland. I can speak about this today only because I am protected by my union."

Embarrassed by the front-page racist ticketing story, the city made ticketing policy changes and an investigation into additional ticketing malfeasance ensued. The deep-ditched parking-division steward was sprung from the hole. The Monday Night Crew had their first major victories.

Among the Monday Night Crew were stewards who could spot any contract violation, who could file successful grievances and civil service board appeals, and who lived to march on the boss. That is how I got to know dreadlocked Brother A, who filed grievances only to have them disappear under the watch of the de facto president and his sidekick. The Monday Night Crew decided to file a ULP charge against the union for failing to represent them when their files went missing.

ULP charges are usually filed by unions against employers, almost never by union members against their union. The seminal duty of fair representation case was brought and won against unions by the late Supreme Court justice Thurgood Marshall who sued white unions for failing to represent their Black members. Word of the filing got upstairs. The newly merged regional Bay Area union could not have it look like it was failing to represent its majority Black and Brown City of Oakland members.

I came to work one day and found, piled high on my desk in three distinct stacks, all the files that Brother A and the Monday Night Crew had been looking for.

Only my new supervisor and the cleaning lady had keys to my office. Neither knew how the files had gotten there. I had the files copied, called the Monday Night Crew, and put the originals in the trunk of my car.

The City of Oakland street sweepers also knew something wasn't right, shutting down city street sweeping regularly and to great effect. I negotiated the terms of at least one street sweeper wildcat strike. Brother T not only shut down street sweeping when necessary but also had my back during disciplinary investigations against me that went nowhere as a result of his help.

Not long after the Bay Area merger, the international union took over a separate, one-hundred-thousand-plus-member statewide California health care union by imposing a trustee-ship on it. Based in Oakland, trustee dissidents opposed to the takeover launched attacks on the international union and loyal affiliates, resulting in public exposés, the removal of city union leaders up and down California, and jail time for some.

The trustee dissidents' campaign against the international union made financial and democratic transparency urgent. Nobody knew when the last City of Oakland officers' election had been held. Another of my many crimes was to see to it that pursuant to the international union's constitution and bylaws, an election committee was convened to duly elect a president.

The de facto president appointed his sidekick to the committee. For every Monday Night Crew member who joined, the de facto president appointed two of his supporters. This is how we learned about the manipulation of the placement of the ballot boxes so they would go only to the sites where the de facto president could count on votes. Election violations were filed and reported to my new supervisor, who removed me from oversight of the election committee so he could oversee it himself.

The de facto president's sidekick had a vested interest in the de facto president's winning. On more than one occasion, I walked into one of the union offices to find him in a swivel chair with a woman on his lap. His back to the door, his hand on her, he appeared to be groping her. She jumped off his lap and closed her blouse when I opened the door.

"This has got to stop," I told him.

The second time I walked in on him, I reported him to the union personnel office.

"You didn't have to tell on him," the de facto president said.

"Yes, I did," I said. "He can't be doing that shit here."

"He's not doing anything," he insisted.

"Well, whatever he's not doing, he can not do it somewhere else," I replied. Third-floor security cameras had footage of the sidekick kissing women in the lobby.

In the merger shuffle, I got a new supervisor whose job it was to get me in line and to protect the de facto president's lost-time work-release agreement.

He called me into his office.

"Ms. Martinez," he said. He never said my first name. He wore light-blue patent leather shoes, an LA thing I'd come to appreciate about him—he wasn't afraid to flash.

"The membership meetings you are interrupting are the members' meetings," he said, referring to the meetings where I'd begun to correct blatant misrepresentations the de facto president made. "They are not your meetings." His voice raised, he rose up, his hands on his desk, his gold watch in the folds of his deep-brown skin, and leaned over to me. "They are the members' meetings," he repeated.

"Yes," I replied. "I represent the members—all the members."

"Look here," he said. "I don't want to have to move on you."

Just then, my colleague Don stepped in. A tall Amerasian man, Don would sometimes stop in my doorway, throw back a lock of black hair, and smile in a wry, straight line that turned up slightly at the ends of his lips. He wore pastel button-down oxford shirts held together by a silver belt buckle over jeans and motorcycle boots. He was a cultural outlander like I was, a person of color raised early in life in the inner plains. We became colleagues when the union merged with a social-worker union.

"Do you need representation?" Don asked.

I shifted myself against the side of my chair so fast, I hit the chair spindles with my thighs hard enough to rock myself.

"Uh, no, Don, but thanks," I said.

"I'll be in my office if you need me," he told me.

The veins on the supervisor's arms bulged; he pressed himself deeper into his desk. "This is my meeting," he said. "I'll decide who attends."

Shifting my chair back, I stood up to face him as Don closed the door behind him.

"And I'll decide if this meeting is leading to disciplinary action and call a steward if I need one," I said.

I sat back down, my hand over my mouth, and tried not to laugh. The boss had shown his ass and squandered his cool.

"Look," he said, seated now and reaching his arms toward me over his desk. "Man, can't you just try to get along here?"

"I am," I said. "But you know I can't be complicit in any bullshit."

The air smog-thick between us, I got up and, facing him, pushed my chair into his desk.

"Is that all?" I asked.

He waved me off.

I closed the door behind me, leaned against it with my hands one over the other against my back, and felt a buzz up my spine.

Later, in the elevator, the de facto president and his sidekick commenced stare-downs with chest puffing that made the space feel really small. My feet planted in my corner, I held my head cocked up, as the de facto president was a full nine inches taller, and his stretched-out T-shirt girth took up half the elevator door he blocked with it. We kept our eyes fixed on each other all the way down the two floors. The door opened and he blinked.

"Thought so," I said, moving around them.

When Don was outside putting on his motorcycle gear, the supervisor stopped to drop threats on Don. Don and I reported the incidents to each other and started a file on all three of them.

Don loved his motorcycle and was very particular about its maintenance. It was a shock some years later when he died in a motorcycle accident that involved an antelope on some desolate stretch of road. Don Evans was a reps' rep, a union man, and the most gangsta social worker I would ever meet.

The Monday Night Crew had more victories, and it started getting harder for the de facto president to deliver for his city handlers who were feeling the pressure of our campaigns.

Under Brother A and Sister C's leadership, we mobilized a campaign with the city's building inspectors to back off a city plan to water down their job descriptions, a move that would have weakened city inspection standards.

The revenue department sistas, collectively recalling and drawing strength from their families' civil rights heritage, successfully fended off a city management attack on them.

At a monthly membership meeting in a packed public works conference room, the de facto president and his sidekick misrepresented a key political endorsement that benefited the candidate of their choosing. I stood to face the membership and clarified the regional political action committee's actual vote.

After the meeting, the de facto president walked over to me alone and stood close, close enough that I could hear his breathing.

"You have got to go," he said. "I am going to see to it that you are taken care of."

I took out a sheet of paper in front of him with my supervisor in earshot and wrote down what he said, noting the time, date, and place. He left. I looked over at my supervisor.

"I didn't see or hear anything," he said.

Just then, a woman stepped forward. I'll call her Public Works Sista.

"I heard it," she said. "I heard what he said. Here's my contact information. I'll be your witness."

"Thanks," I said. "I'm going to need it."

She'd wanted to get involved in the union, but the de facto president had told her that she was too old and that women didn't belong in the union.

She wasn't the only woman the de facto president discouraged or felt threatened by. Police Division Sista knew the de facto president to be the "fool he was through and through." There was also Dispatch Sista, whose instincts I trusted as I got to know her, and Library Sista, the only white sista to join the Monday Night Crew. Under her leadership, we carried out a city library–wide campaign to issue overdue notices to protest City of Oakland library mismanagement and incompetence.

There have always been angels on this path. They have appeared in the unlikeliest incarnations: Don Evans, all the sistas, the righteous brothers, and the rocks in the sand. It's like whatever grace propelled me forward propelled them forward too, and simultaneously we arose at just the right moment.

One of the last large membership meetings I attended took place at a different union hall, big enough to hold all the major departments. Layoffs were coming. The city had a history of playing fast and loose with contract language to protect favorites and punish enemies. Now it made sense why the deal I intercepted early on between city management and the de facto president was so important: it would have weakened the layoff bumping-rights provisions of the labor contract.

The de facto president sat in front of the room at tables facing the membership. Members from Streets, Sewers, Parking, Downtown, and other departments filed in.

Wood-on-wood gavel.

"Before we get started," the de facto president said, "I'll entertain a motion to have our union rep removed from this meeting. We need to protect her from hearing anything illegal we might plan in our fight against the layoffs. That way, she can preserve deniability in her dealings with the city on our behalf. We're just trying to protect her," he said.

"Do I hear a motion?"

Wood-on-wood gavel.

It was a benevolent pronouncement that betrayed malintent the likes of which I'd heard before.

As an undergraduate at the University of Washington, I'd witnessed Philippine president Ferdinand Marcos's henchman Tony Baruso stand up in front of the hundreds who gathered at the International Longshore and Warehouse Union/Local 37 Cannery Workers' Union hall after the murders of union reformers Silme Domingo and Gene Viernes. They were gunned down in broad daylight at the Local 37 offices in Pioneer Square in Seattle in 1981.

Baruso called for prayers for Silme and Gene and their families and vowed to get to the bottom of the murders. Everybody knew he was implicated. Later litigation would tie the murders directly to the Marcos regime, and Baruso would die in prison for his involvement.

As former UW students and community activists, Silme and Gene had involved student activists in Local 37 reform efforts. As Chicano student activists, we forged alliances with Filipino university-student activists who worked summers on the cannery boats.

When the University of Washington, the equivalent of the California UC system, tried to close admission to working-class students and students of color under pressure from affluent parents whose kids were being denied admission, we mobilized. Inspired by Silme and Gene, we shut down university buildings and all went to jail together, Blacks, Latinos, Asians, poor whites, and Native peoples. There is a UW *Daily* front-page picture of me in handcuffs being hauled out of Schmitz Hall.

Wood-on-wood gavel.

A member rose up and looked over at me and said, "She don't look like she needs protecting to me. We want her in this meeting."

Foot stomping. Loud clapping. A member from the seats shouted, "We de ones need protecting, muffkr . . . from yo ass."

The room erupted. The de facto president gaveled. A member stood and addressed me directly.

"Sister Yvonne," he said, "do you need to leave this meeting for your own protection?"

"No, Brother," I said. "I'm feelin' pretty safe right here, right now."

Another member stood.

"Yeah, besides, meaning no disrespect to you, Mr. President,

Yvonne is our rep, and we need her advice and counsel now that the city is about to make its usual crooked moves with the layoffs."

The sidekick, who had been sitting in front of the room, quickly moved to the back as the tide against the de facto president started to turn. The de facto president sent a message to his sidekick. "Call her boss," he mouthed.

The de facto president talked about having to leave his wife at home with their new baby son, said she'd just gotten home from the hospital and was in bed and bleeding when he left. A masterful deflection, I thought, even if it was at his poor wife's expense, an attempt to engender sympathy with a graphic visual to break the momentum of the meeting.

A member of the Monday Night Crew stood and spread his gaze thickly over the room to silence it. "Mr. President," he said, "belated congratulations on the birth of your baby son."

Bumpy groans all around. He looked around again, and the room went flatline quiet.

"With all due respect, Mr. President, perhaps you should be at home with your wife and baby son and your vice president should take over this meeting."

The room erupted again.

Just then, upon a signal from the sidekick in the back of the room, the president gaveled for a ten-minute recess. The meeting broke out into the hallway, inside and outside the room.

My supervisor arrived. "Ms. Martinez," he said, in a straight-up-and-down ghetto stare-down. We stood there, caught between his unstated *I-can't-wait-to-whip-your-ass* stance and my unstated *Oh-but-bring-it-if-you-can* response.

The détente held until the Monday Night Crew secured their agenda and made it clear that I wasn't going anywhere.

On one of my last follow-the-dog searches, I went looking for the bargaining book, which had gone missing. The bargaining book is a record of the proposal exchanges between the parties during successors' union contract negotiations. It records the notes, the discussion, and the intent behind proposed contract language changes and keeps track of the most minute language variations, even down to the movement or omission of a comma. It is the union's legal record of the final labor contract agreement and is kept by the union's chief spokesperson, the union's agent at the bargaining table.

The de facto president didn't have it; his sidekick, who had access to all kinds of information, didn't have it; and no member of the bargaining team had it. Files, offices, drawers, shelves were searched. The support staff checked the archives. Nothing—no book, no box of notes, no draft proposals. Nothing.

To legal geeks like me, the bargaining book was the holy grail. With pending layoffs, I had to see what kind of record the negotiated labor agreement had preserved.

One day, on some obscure shelf in an unsecured conference room, there it was, half-open, its pages in disarray. I pulled it down and examined the cover insert to confirm what it was.

"Is this it?" I asked.

"Oh, you found it," the de facto president said.

"Yeah," I replied.

"Yeah," he said. "That's it."

Every chief spokesperson has their own method for preserving the record of contract negotiations. The order of the book made no sense, and some pages were missing.

The former chief spokesperson, who'd bargained the contract, was a crony of the union executive board member who'd kicked me out of Berkeley, tried to get me fired, and likened organizing to "the Devil." After months of bargaining, he couldn't close the contract, so he bargained the lost-time work-release side deal, with all its perks and benefits, for the de facto president, who then muscled the entire settlement through the bargaining team under protest by Brother A.

I got a copy of that agreement when it was time to renew it, only to have it disappear from my office. With no line of union authority over the de facto president, the former chief spokesperson bought a contract settlement by selling off accountability, thereby handing the City of Oakland chapter over to the de facto president and the city management/union's former chief of staff, who had an axe to grind. The de facto president came to power in a payoff.

Ultimately, the de facto president won the stacked election. He promised "I willed you here" Parking Deputy Sista that if he won, he would see to it that I stayed in Oakland no matter what happened and that we would continue our campaigns against the city. She mobilized the parking deputies to support his campaign.

The morning after his election, I congratulated the new president. Though tainted in this instance, City of Oakland chapter elections were now in place.

After months of acrimony, the new president embraced me. He was now legit, sort of—or more legit than he had been, anyway. He bought himself a camel hair overcoat and walked city hall, his briefcase in hand and his sidekick in tow. It was a Pyrrhic victory.

The newly merged Bay Area union had an election of its own.

When emails to the directors above my supervisor went unanswered, I emailed the union's newly elected executive team, sharing what I'd learned about the newly elected City of Oakland chapter president's special arrangement and outlining potential liabilities for the union.

I came to work one day, ready to steel myself against a gauntlet of abuse. Outside, Don's motorcycle was gone. All the lights down the hall were off but one. I knocked.

"Come in, come in," my colleague said. "Shut the door." Her voice cracked low, like hard bread.

"What's up? Where is everybody?" I asked.

"He's gone. He had to go back to the yard," she replied.

"What?" I said.

"Yeah, girl, he gone," she repeated. "His lost-time deal is over."

"When?" I asked.

"Don't know," she said. "Girl, what did you do?"

Whatever I said must have been loud.

She put her hands on my arms. "Shush," she told me. "Keep it down."

My arms braced, she held me while I jumped up and down.

I sidewinded my way out of there and back up the hall, Spidey like, my arms wide, my palms and backside against the wall and empty offices.

I sent a notice to the union's personnel office detailing the months of harassment, along with a witness list. As before, when I complained about my City of San of Francisco boss harasser, they moved me, not the harasser. I was transferred to a county sixty miles away. I was banned from Oakland and from Occupy Oakland.

I was put in what I called the rep protection program. My new secretary was told to tell any member who called for me that I wasn't there. I was prohibited from returning any calls that managed to get through and from directly contacting anyone at the City of Oakland chapter.

The sistas and brothers started a campaign to find me and return me to Oakland.

To this day, I've had no contact with Brother A, who won the election two years later. In January of 2013, Sister C, his vice president, wrote on my Facebook page when no one could find me. I cherish the message to this day.

Hi Yvonne, long time no see/hear. All is well and the fight is alive and kickin' with the city and others. I'll keep you posted. We miss you a whole lot. Take care and keep on fighting the good fight and don't let anyone change that, no matter what happens. Thank you for all that you've done for us. It is truly appreciated. Love you.

When things died down, I went back to Oakland to support a different chapter, the Port of Oakland workers' strike. I wore huge dark glasses and a hoodie. One of the City of Oakland brothers saw me.

"Yvonne, when you coming back? We need you in Oakland right now," he said.

My cover blown, I thanked him, clasped his hands in mine, and headed for my car to, as a friend said, slip back up to the Sierra.

The Monday Night Crew won the following election. I was told I would be returned to Oakland. I waited, but it never happened.

AFTERWORD

My great-grandfather defied a Mormon posse. My grandmother, his daughter, organized against greedy tavern owners. My great grandmother survived the threat of a mob after my great grandfather was killed as a bandit by the Mormons. All these acts of resistance influenced me as much as the transgenerational trauma they passed down. As an organizer/activist, writing these essays and doing the work to unlock the trauma, I found that hidden sources of resistance and resilience were unlocked too. I posit that trauma and resistance, like a double helix are bound together and are both passed down. That a healing journey unlocks both. Daring to look, daring to heal and daring to act is revolutionary.

ACKNOWLEDGMENTS

I want to thank all the women who came to believe in themselves enough to dare to write down their first line and then the next and the next until their journey took them to freedom.

Special thanks to my daughter, Andrea, whose steady and unwavering love inspire gratitude and joy. To my son, Ruben, who inspires hope. To my niece fan base, Rachie and Bianca for knowing and believing. Thanks to my late aunt Vicki Contente for her invaluable research and lifelong kindness.

Abrazos calurosos to my OG Organizer Sisters: Ana, Eleanor, and Suzanne.

Thanks to my many friends who read my stories and came to my readings, Barbara, Alice, Marcia. Thanks to Bre for her insightful observations. Thanks to the Mexican Coffee Shop guys who served me coffee with a story or joke, los agradezco mucho.

Special thanks to Tom Spanbauer and the Dangerous writers who met in his Portland basement week after week to learn the craft of writing.

Big thanks go to She Writes Press and all the staff, without whom this book would not have happened, including editor Annie Tucker who came to love my grandmother as much as I did, and to editors Katie Caruana and Elizabeth Kaufman for their diligent follow through.

ABOUT THE AUTHOR

Yvonne Martinez is a retired labor negotiator/organizer. She has been published by *ZyZZyVa, Crab Orchard Review, Labor Notes,* and *NPR.* She also formerly wrote a local labor blog in the San Francisco Bay Area. Her memoir in essays, *Someday Mija, You'll Learn the Difference Between a Whore and a Working Woman,* covers her childhood in Salt Lake City/South Central/Boyle Heights and her work as a labor negotiator/organizer in California and the Pacific Northwest. Her play *Scabmuggers* is based on her experience as a National Fellow of the Harvard Trade Union Program in 1994. Yvonne lives in Berkeley, CA, and Portland, OR.

Author photo © Matt Wong

SELECTED TITLES FROM SHE WRITES PRESS

She Writes Press is an independent publishing company founded to serve women writers everywhere. Visit us at www.shewritespress.com.

Singing with the Sirens: Overcoming the Long-Term Effects of Childhood Sexual Exploitation by Ellyn Bell and Stacey Bell. $16.95, 978-1-63152-936-8. With metaphors of sea creatures and the force of the ocean as a backdrop, this work addresses the problems of sexual abuse and exploitation of young girls, taking the reader on a poetic journey toward finding healing from within.

Baffled by Love: Stories of the Lasting Impact of Childhood Trauma Inflicted by Loved Ones by Laurie Kahn. $16.95, 978-1-63152-226-0. For three decades, Laurie Kahn has treated clients who were abused as children—people who were injured by someone who professed to love them. Here, she shares stories from her own rocky childhood along with those of her clients, weaving a textured tale of the all-too-human search for the "good kind of love."

Fortunate Daughter: A Memoir of Reconciliation by Rosie McMahan. $16.95, 978-1-64742-024-6. Intimate, unsentimental, and inspiring, this memoir explores the journey of one woman from abused little girl to healed adult, even as she maintains her relationship with her former abuser.

Now I Can See the Moon: A Story of a Social Panic, False Memories, and a Life Cut Short by Alice Tallmadge. $16.95, 978-1-63152-330-4. A first-person account from inside the bizarre and life-shattering social panic over child sex abuse that swept through the US in the 1980s— and affected Alice Tallmadge's family in a personal, devastating way.

Say It Out Loud: Revealing and Healing the Scars of Sexual Abuse by Roberta Dolan. $16.95, 978-1-938314-99-5. An in-depth guide to healing the wounds caused by sexual abuse, written by a survivor who's lived the process firsthand.

Secrets in Big Sky Country: A Memoir by Mandy Smith. $16.95, 978-1-63152-814-9. A bold and unvarnished memoir about the shattering consequences of familial sexual abuse—and the strength it takes to overcome them.